THE CHICAGO "L"

Mundelein College students Betty Venhorst and Beatrice Deyerling pay their fares to cashier Ella Whalen for an "L" ride in 1936. Join them for one of the best rides in America. (Chicago History Museum.)

On the front cover: The original Chicago "L" station house (on Chicago Avenue) still serves passengers on what is now the Brown Line. This photograph was taken shortly after the ornate station opened in 1900. A competing streetcar line runs by on the right. The large building in the background foreshadows monumental changes for the "L"—and all of society: the Rambler Bicycle factory, home of a company about to begin manufacturing automobiles. (Chicago Transit Authority.)

On the back cover: Frank Sprague (second from left) tests his multiple-unit train control on the South Side "L" in 1898. This technology, first put to work in Chicago, allowed one train operator to control several motorized transit cars from any operating cab. It vastly improved "L" operations. (Chicago Transit Authority.)

THE CHICAGO "L"

Greg Borzo

Published by Arcadia Publishing
Charleston SC, Chicago IL, Portsmouth NH, San Francisco CA

Printed in the United States of America

Library of Congress Catalog Card Number: 2007923200

For all general information contact Arcadia Publishing at:
Telephone 843-853-2070
Fax 843-853-0044
E-mail sales@arcadiapublishing.com
For customer service and orders:
Toll-Free 1-888-313-2665

Visit us on the Internet at www.arcadiapublishing.com

To my wife, Christine Bertrand, who helped with this book every step of the way, always patient, generous, and supportive. Also to my big brother, Paul, who instilled in me a fondness for trains and a love of writing.

CONTENTS

ACKNOWLEDGMENTS

The most remarkable thing about working on this book was the way scores of people—friends and strangers, alike—jumped at the chance to contribute, whether by providing photographs and feedback or by answering questions and offering to proofread. I am deeply grateful to all of these generous individuals. Their enthusiasm for this project can only be attributed to the widespread interest in and affection for the "L," one of Chicago's most engaging assets.

Thanks are due, first and foremost, to the Chicago Transit Authority (CTA), which was extremely accommodating in making available its rich photographic collection. Particularly helpful was Bruce Moffat, CTA historian and photo archivist, but Cindy Kaitcer, Noelle Gaffney, and Joyce Shaw also lent valuable assistance.

Early on, I was fortunate to plug into a network of transit experts, in particular Art Peterson and Roy Benedict, who guided me throughout the project. I learned a tremendous amount from them—not just about "L" history and operations, but more importantly about helping others openhandedly.

Many others helped just as willingly, including proofreaders par excellence Frank Malone and Paul Borzo. Attorney Amy Cook provided legal and publishing advice. And Pat Kremer at the Field Museum offered unflinching support and encouragement.

Of course many of these key supporters helped in multiple ways: Bruce opened his personal collection as well as that of the CTA, Art and Roy proofread drafts as well as being expert sounding boards, Frank and Paul provided advice about the photographs, as well as proofreading.

So many people helped me gather the more than 260 photographs that went into this book (and countless others that did not make the cut) that I cannot mention them all. Especially helpful were Walter Keevil at the CTA; Christine Giannoni at the Field Museum; Meg Givhan at the Chicago Department of Cultural Affairs; Michael Dorf at Adducci, Dorf, Lehner, Mitchell, and Blankenship; Josh Gartler at Poster Plus; Richard Dreiser at the Yerkes Observatory; photographer Terry Evans; Kristin Standaert at the Illinois Institute of Technology; Julie Lynch at the Chicago Public Library; Joan Metzger at Northern Illinois University; William Massa at the Yale University Library; and Frank Carlson at the Villa Park Historical Society.

John Pearson and Melissa Basilone, my publisher and editor (respectively) at Arcadia Publishing, are to be commended for their patience, professionalism, and problem-solving skills. I would also like to thank established Arcadia author Lori Grove for introducing me to them.

None of this would have happened, however, without the Chicago History Museum, whose exhibits and interpreter training program ignited the spark that was my interest in local history. The entire museum staff and volunteer corps are to be applauded, but I would like to specifically acknowledge Marne Bariso, Ginny Fitzgerald, Russell Lewis, Lesley Martin, and Rob Medina.

Finally, I must recognize a few giants of Chicago history and/or the "L" scene who helped me understand the subject, in detail and in terms of its broader context. These authors of books, videos, tours, and Web sites helped me through their works and in person: Perry Duis, Graham Garfield, Geoffrey Baer, and, again, Bruce Moffat and Art Peterson.

Thank you all so very much. Let us hope our collective efforts will benefit our venerable "L" and the city it serves so tirelessly.

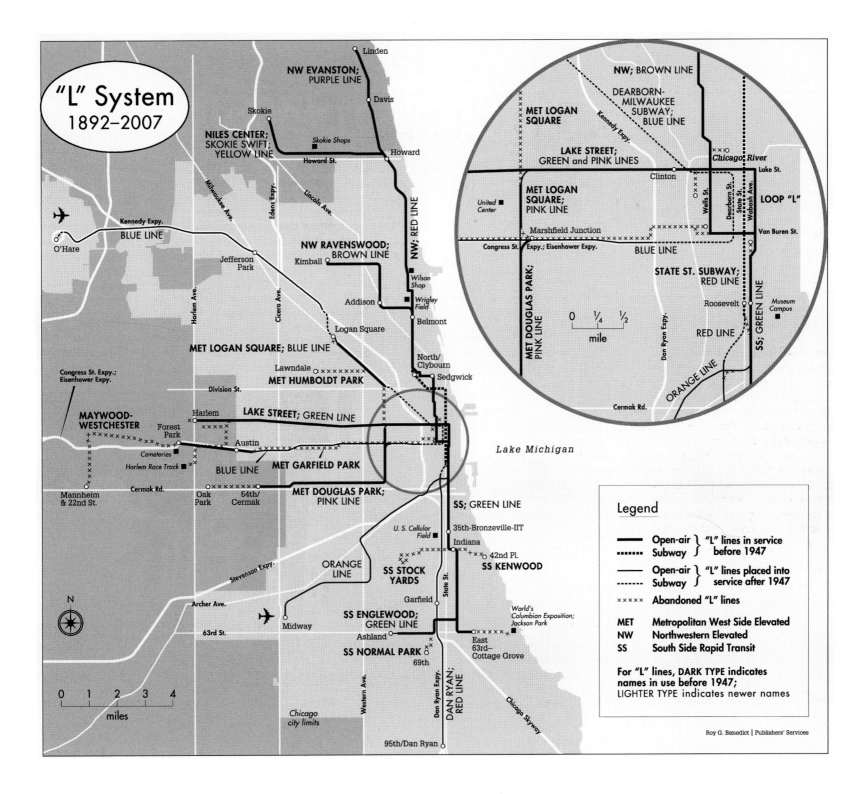

"L" System 1892–2007

SS NORMAL PARK

Roy G. Benedict | Publishers' Services

Legend

	"L" lines in service before 1947
Open-air	
Subway	

	"L" lines placed into service after 1947
Open-air	
Subway	

××××× Abandoned "L" lines

MET Metropolitan West Side Elevated
NW Northwestern Elevated
SS South Side Rapid Transit

For "L" lines, DARK TYPE indicates names in use before 1947;
LIGHTER TYPE indicates newer names

New cars tour the property in 1976, crossing the Chicago River on the Lake Street double-deck bridge. The Merchandise Mart and Marina City towers stand in the background. (CTA.)

FOREWORD

In 1890, Chicago boasted a population of 1,099,850. By itself this is not a particularly remarkable number, yet it registered astonishment around the world. The reason was simple—between 1830 and 1890, Chicago was the fastest-growing city on the globe. Its population increased almost 37 times during those 60 years, and its borders expanded rapidly as well.

This explosive growth came as the result of a remarkable fusion of two powerful 19th-century juggernauts: urbanization and industrialization. In Chicago each reinforced the other and transformed the city into a national crossroads, a position tied to the intersection of far-reaching waterways and rail lines that connected the continent and converged in the city.

But the 1890s also brought a stark reminder of the perils of urbanization, the city was literally choking on its own success. Crowding and traffic congestion were vexing obstacles to commerce and to making Chicago livable. One solution was to build up. While the story of Chicago's skyscrapers is well known, the "L," the other built-up structure, is often taken for granted or even regarded as a nuisance. Yet its significance cannot be overstated. The "L" gave Chicago's one million–plus inhabitants rapid and easy access to large parts of the city. Equally important, the "L" spurred neighborhood development, pulling outlying areas of the city's expanded boundaries into closer orbit around the Loop.

The "L" has a unique place in Chicago today. It reveals the choices made and deals struck beginning more than 115 years ago. It remains a vital part of contemporary city life, a system that has been modified to meet the ongoing needs of a dynamic population and a regional metropolitan area. Born in the crucible of Chicago's urban prospects and problems, the "L" survives and thrives as a quintessential and enduring feature of the city's ever-changing landscape.

—Russell Lewis
Executive Vice President and Chief Historian, Chicago History Museum

 # CHICAGO "L" TIMELINE

1890

1892 South Side Rapid Transit, Chicago's 1st "L"
1893 Worlds Fair pioneers electric third-rail system
1893 Lake Street Elevated, the second "L"
1895 Metropolitan West Side Elevated, the third "L"
1897 Union Loop connects first three "L" lines

1900

1900 Northwestern Elevated, the fourth "L"
1903-47 Newspaper trains operate to suburbs
1906-34 Charter funeral trains to western suburbs
1906 Last horse cars and cable cars run
1907 Ravenswood Branch opens on Northwest Side

1910

1911 Chicago Elevated Railways takes over four "Ls"
1913 CER introduces transfers, through routes
1914 "L" buys first steel-bodied cars
1918 Worldwide flu epidemic prompts smoking ban
1918 After 26 years, original five-cent fare increases

1920

1920–73 "L" operates freight service
1924 Four "Ls" united as Chicago Rapid Transit
1926 "L" carries record 229 million passengers

1930

1930s Depression hits "L" hard, ridership falls
1938 Construction begins on two subways

1940

1943 State subway opens, despite WWII
1943-48 Number of stations peaks at 227
1945 Chicago Transit Authority created
1948 CTA starts streamlining, closes branches
1948–95 CTA runs A/B skip-stop service

1950

1950–99 Tokens accepted to pay fares
1951 Partially complete Dearborn subway opens
1957 Last wooden "L" cars retired
1958 Last streetcars retired
1958 "L" opens in Congress Expressway median

1960

1961 CTA inaugurates one-person crews
1963 Last interurban stops operating on "L"
1964 Air-conditioned "L" cars become common
1969 Dan Ryan "L" opens in highway median

1970

1973 Regional Transit Authority created as overseer
1974 CTA hires first women conductors
1977 Loop "L" experiences most notorious accident
1977 Clarke House moved over tracks, gets stuck

1980

1984 "L" extended to O'Hare International Airport
1988 Quincy station renovated to 1897 appearance

1990

1993 CTA introduces color-coded names for lines
1993 Orange Line opens to Midway Airport
1996 Huge fire destroys Wilson Shop
1997 Pay-on-train discontinued

2000

2000 Use of conductors discontinued
2000 CTA allows two bikes per "L" car
2006 Pink Line opens
2006 Museum puts first "L" car on display
2007 "Year of Decision" for Chicago "L"

INTRODUCTION

From 1892 to 1900—in a flurry of enthusiasm for the emerging technology of elevated rail transit—engineers and entrepreneurs, tycoons and laborers built four "L" lines. They used a new, riveted plate-steel construction technology that had been perfected a few years earlier on the Eiffel Tower. Construction cost $500,000 to $1 million per mile, now about $12 million to $24 million per mile, adjusted for inflation. These original "L"s radiated from a bustling but increasingly congested downtown into surrounding residential and industrial areas, farms, and fields. They served as the backbone for additional lines over the following century, creating one of the world's greatest transit systems.

This "High Line" running above the crowded streets on a structure resembling a giant erector set helped to build both a dense, concentrated downtown and a "City of Neighborhoods," as Chicago is known. Over the years the "L" led and followed the city's growth. Today it includes 1,200 rapid transit cars carrying 160 million passengers per year on eight lines serving 144 stations stretching over 222 miles of main-line track.

The "L" is the envy of many cities because of its vital historical role and because it carries half a million riders a day—most of them swiftly and safely—all the while enhancing property values along its routes. It is worth untold billions of dollars.

As soon as the "L" began carrying passengers, however, some people opposed the system, calling it noisy and dangerous, unsightly and unsafe. In 1897, the New York Academy of Medicine warned that elevated trains "prevented the normal development of children, threw convalescing patients into relapses, and caused insomnia, exhaustion, hysteria, paralysis, meningitis, deafness, and death."

Actually, one reason the "L" was elevated was to promote safety and preserve lives. In 1893, Chicago had 1,500 railroad grade crossings that led to hundreds of deaths and injuries. The city forced many railroads to elevate their tracks and required the "L" to be elevated, right from the start, as a safety measure. Nevertheless, fears and economic factors generated several campaigns to tear down parts of the "L." In fact, more than eight miles of Chicago's elevated track structure have been demolished (and many more miles of track at ground level and on embankments have been abandoned or ripped up). As recently as 1979, half of the Loop "L" was scheduled to be replaced.

Today the long-term future of this remarkable system seems secure. The "L" is under tremendous financial strain, but just one "L" train can keep hundreds of automobiles off the street, and that means a lot in this era of rising gasoline prices and concerns about global warming.

The best way to experience Chicago is via the "L," which offers a ride through an unparalleled urban landscape. As the "L" thunders past skyscrapers and vacant lots, beautiful parks and messy backyards, churches and saloons, the journey can very much be the destination. This book may inspire such journeys, but as you read it, please bear in mind two things: First, when a name refers to a street it will say so, as in "Roosevelt Road"; on the other hand, "Roosevelt" by itself refers to an "L" station. Second, this book is meant to be read in the order in which it is presented. It compresses the long, sometimes complicated history of the "L" into a series of captions and photographs in chronological order.

So pay your fare and jump on board for a ride through the history and mystery of the "L," Chicago's most stirring, democratic, and historical form of transportation.

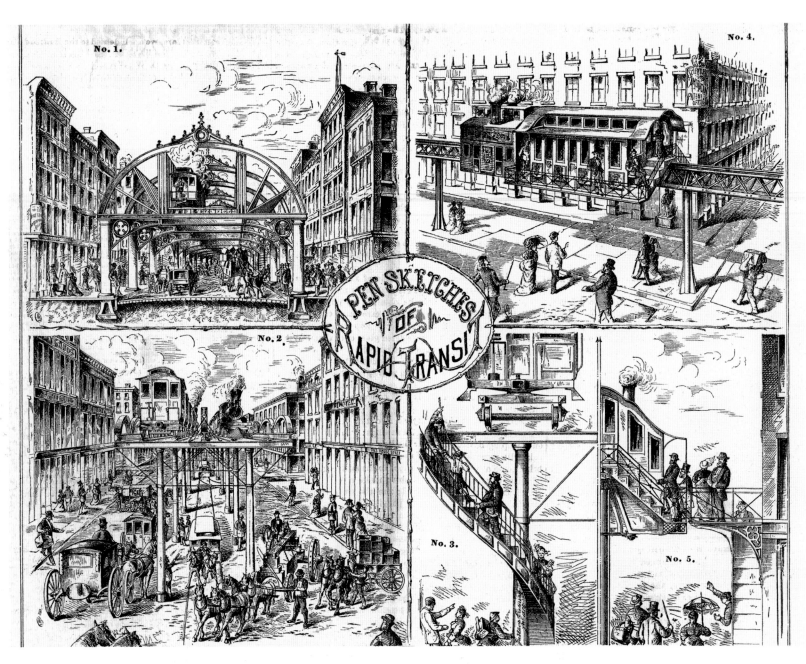

In the late 1800s, there was no shortage of ideas for elevated
rapid transit systems. (*Scientific American.*)

Opposite: Chicago's first transit mode was the omnibus. Many were former stagecoaches put out of intercity transportation
service by the growth of railroads; within the city, most were used to transport railroad passengers to other train stations or
hotels. In 1853, Frank Parmelee started Chicago's first fixed-route omnibus service. Here immigrants disembark a Parmelee
omnibus in the 1850s at the Chicago and North Western Railway's Immigrant Passenger Station on Kinzie Street, half a
block west of that line's main terminal at Kinzie and Wells Streets. (Northern Illinois University Archives.)

PRECURSORS AND PROTOTYPES

The story of the "L" begins with a quick look at various forms of transit that preceded it, whether practical or fanciful, successful or doomed.

When Chicago was incorporated in 1837, most people could readily walk anywhere in the small frontier settlement. Growth, however, increased distances to be traveled. In those horse-and-buggy days, only the wealthy could afford either, so the need for transit arose.

For much of the second half of the 19th century, Chicago was the world's fastest-growing city. As it grew, downtown traffic congestion became intolerable. Something had to be done to get people to and through the city center. At the same time, Chicago was widely considered to be the place where the future was unfolding. Therefore, much of the experimentation in transit that took place around the world was centered in brash, bold Chicago.

Throughout this period, inventors and entrepreneurs, as well as a few crackpots, promoted everything from monorails to moving sidewalks. They bombarded the city with schemes and dreams for public conveyances to be pushed or pulled by horses, stationary steam engines, water pressure, pneumatic power, gas motors, locomotives, electricity, batteries, rope, compressed air, and even sail. The successful systems were the omnibus in 1853; horse-drawn railcar in 1859; cable car in 1882; electric trolley in 1890; and "L" in 1892. This chapter explores some of these myriad innovations, winners and losers.

Omnibuses were uncomfortable and traveled slowly over rutted, muddy, or dusty streets. Horse cars—offering a quicker, smoother ride on rails—began to compete with them in 1859. A driver and conductor from the West Chicago Street Railroad pose in front of their Van Buren Street horsecar in 1891. Full-sized cars required two horses and averaged about six miles an hour. (CTA.)

Horses were expensive, created a mess, needed to be fed, were subject to disease, and could work only a few hours a day. Transit companies sought alternatives such as the steam locomotive, but the smoke and noise it produced spooked horses and annoyed people. This one on Evanston Avenue (now Broadway) in 1864 was disguised as a car to appear less threatening and was called a "dummy" to imply that it made no noise. (CTA, George Krambles collection.)

In Chicago, the first successful alternative to horse power was the cable car, which could run twice as fast but cost only half as much to operate. After adoption in San Francisco starting in 1873, the cable car came to Chicago in 1882 and caught on quickly. The technology that had conquered steep hills also could master level, straight streets. Emerging transit baron Charles Tyson Yerkes aggressively converted his major horsecar lines to cable from 1887 to 1893. Chicago then had 1,500 cable cars, 11 power stations, and 86 miles of track—the largest cable car system in the world (in terms of vehicles and passengers but not miles). This North Chicago Street Railroad train of cable cars ran from downtown to Clark Street and Schubert Avenue near what was then the northern city limit. (CTA.)

Next came trolleys, streetcars powered by electricity drawn from overhead wires. Popularized in 1888, trolleys reached Chicago in 1890. This robust motorman runs his North Chicago Electric Railway trolley in 1900 past wooden sidewalks, wagons, and mud. Many people feared the wires, especially downtown, but by 1906 the trolley had driven horsecars and cable cars out of business. (CTA, George Krambles collection.)

Thousands of transit vehicles, wagons, horses, and pedestrians competed for space in Chicago's increasingly congested downtown. When traffic delays became intolerable, politicians and the public realized that new transit lines were needed above or below the fray. The high cost of subways meant building up, but how? There was no shortage of ideas. *Scientific American* published this design: a car suspended under a locomotive. (*Scientific American.*)

Manhattan built the country's first elevated rail transit system, the West Side and Yonkers Patent Railway. On December 7, 1867, Charles Harvey demonstrated the safety of his invention for company directors, potential investors, and onlookers by riding a handcar on a half-mile track over Greenwich Street from Battery Place at the southern tip of Manhattan north to Morris Street. (Collection of the New-York Historical Society, 15129.)

Charles Harvey's innovative elevated rail transit system in Manhattan was also the country's first cable car transit line. Car-pulling cables running along the track were driven by steam engines buried underground every 1,500 feet or so. This 1869 view south on Greenwich Street from Little West 12th Street shows the boxy, circular enclosure that housed the cable. The single-track line, suspended by what looks like a rickety line of single posts, began revenue service in the summer of 1868. *Harpers Weekly* reported, "The rapid speed attained . . . leads friends of the enterprise to hope that the problem of rapid and safe locomotion through the crowded streets of the city has been solved." The line was extended north to 30th Street and operated until 1870, when it was abandoned. In 1871, it was reopened as a steam locomotive line. (Collection of the New-York Historical Society, 3253.)

One of Chicago's first elevated railroads carried freight rather than people. In September 1892, a three-and-a-half-mile line at the Union Stock Yards began hauling supplies around the Armour meatpacking plant. Here in 1892, a five-car train runs on track passing alongside—and supported by—buildings. Single-axle cars were pulled by small electric locomotives (inset) powered from an overhead wire. The system operated until 1920. (Bruce Moffat collection.)

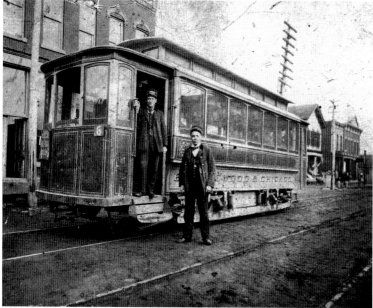

One of the many forms of transit motive power that did not take hold in the 19th century was battery power. The Englewood and Chicago Electric Street Railway operated this "storage battery car" from 1896 to 1901 between Sixty-third Street and Blue Island or Mount Greenwood. (CTA.)

By far, Chicago's most innovative elevated railroad of this era was the Columbian Intramural Railway, which carried fairgoers at the World's Columbian Exposition of 1893. Remarkably it was the first elevated rail line in the world to use the uncovered, trackside, third-rail electrical power system that the "L" uses to this day. (Paul V. Galvin Library, Illinois Institute of Technology.)

SECTION OF THE INTRAMURAL ROAD.

20

An electric motorized car at the fair pulls three unpowered cars along the lakefront. The colonnade connecting the agricultural and machinery buildings (inset) housed one of the Columbian Intramural Railway's 10 stations, as seen from the lettering above its center portico. (Paul V. Galvin Library, Illinois Institute of Technology.)

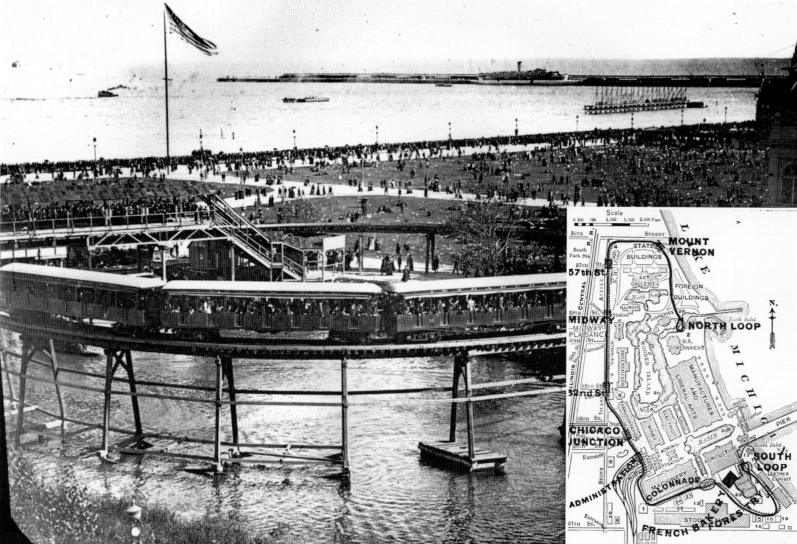

The Columbian Intramural Railway's three-mile route (inset) had turning loops at each end, and this photograph shows the north loop. The railway was quite successful, carrying almost six million people without any fatalities during the six months the fair was open. It was torn down soon after the fair closed on October 31, 1893. Add "L" technology to the long list of innovations—from Cracker Jacks to the Ferris wheel—attributable to the incredible World's Columbian Exposition. (Bruce Moffat collection.)

Opposite: Construction of the South Side "L" began in February 1890. Men wearing bowlers rather than hard hats position a connecting span at Thirty-fifth Street, aided by a steam-powered traveling crane. While elevated lines in New York ran above city streets, the South Side "L" was built mostly above private land alongside alleys. This avoided the difficulty of obtaining property owners' consent to use their street. It also earned the nickname of the Alley "L." (CTA.)

FIRST "L"—SOUTH SIDE

From 1867, when Manhattan began operating the Greenwich Street elevated line, until 1900, 70 proposals for an elevated rail line were introduced in Chicago (which even then had a "Second City" complex). One plan called for a line through downtown buildings. Nothing came of all this talk until the chance to host a world's fair presented itself in the mid-1880s.

If Chicago was to win the fair, it would need better transit than plodding horsecars and a few crowded cable cars. As talk of getting the highly sought-after fair grew more promising, the Chicago and South Side Rapid Transit, the city's first "L" line, was incorporated in 1888. The first leg of this "L" was to run from a terminal at Congress Street near State Street south to Thirty-ninth Street, then the southern border of the city. When Chicago annexed 125 square miles (partly to improve its case to host the fair) in 1889, extending the line became likely.

In 1890, the U.S. Congress voted to hold the World's Columbian Exposition in Chicago, and the city decided to locate the fair in Jackson Park on the far Southeast Side. Plans were quickly drawn up to extend the "L" south to Sixty-third Street and then east to Jackson Park. Along Sixty-third Street it ran above the middle of the street, which was so sparsely developed that few businesses and property owners objected. The line's first leg to Thirty-ninth Street opened in 1892 and the second to Jackson Park the following year.

A group of engineers who worked on the foundation of the Alley "L" pose in 1890 with some of their tools. In many cases, property had to be condemned to secure the right-of-way from people or businesses who did not want to sell, or who demanded exorbitant payoffs. (CTA.)

Chicago's first "L" operated with steam locomotives. In 1892, these 20 "little engines that could" left the Baldwin Locomotive Works in Philadelphia for Chicago. Their diminutive size is clear in comparison to the classic main-line steam locomotive hauling them. These locomotives were an improvement over those used on Manhattan's elevated line and were even put on display at the World's Columbian Exposition. (CTA.)

Steam power is not well suited for transit. Locomotives have to build up steam to work efficiently, while transit requires many starts and stops. Operations average only 15 miles per hour, including stops. And locomotives spew smoke and soot, even though the franchise of the Alley "L" required its locomotives to be "fully equipped with all modern devices calculated to render [them] practically noiseless and smokeless." (CTA.)

The new line ordered 180 wooden passenger cars, each 46 feet long and 42,500 pounds. They were beautifully crafted with gold leaf trim, mahogany interiors, slatted shades, gas lamps, a canvas-over-wood roof, and colored-glass ventilator windows along the roof. South Side Rapid Transit Car 1 ran in revenue service from 1892 to 1930, and its open platform must have provided quite a ride. It is now on display at the Chicago History Museum. (CTA.)

When the South Side "L" opened to the public on June 6, 1892, it ran 3.6 miles between Congress and Thirty-ninth Streets. The trip cost 5¢ and took 14 minutes—half the time it took cable cars on State Street to cover the same distance. Its proximity to the backs of houses and apartment buildings along the way afforded riders a peek inside homes, exposing "bits of domestic life usually hidden from the gaze of passing crowds," as one reporter put it. The original South Side "L" station houses were at ground level, like this one at Fortieth Street, looking east at Indiana Avenue. All the original station houses have been demolished except the one at Garfield Boulevard, although it is no longer in service. (CTA.)

The South Side "L" reached the fair on May 12, 1893, 11 days after the fair opened. This view of the fair's rail terminal looks northeast across Stony Island Avenue. Main-line railroads arrived via the curved tracks on the right. The South Side "L" terminal is behind the large, towered Cold Storage Building on the left. The "L" connected with the Columbian Intramural Railway, which ran across the scene and crossed the main-line tracks just in front of the Central Railroad Station on the right. The South Side "L" carried more than 12 million passengers to the fair, even though the event was also served by cable cars, electric trolleys, shore boats, and main-line railroads. (Chicago History Museum.)

After the fair, ridership plummeted, forcing the Alley "L" into receivership in 1895. A continuing problem was the lack of development on the southern portion of the line, as seen in this 1896 view of a southbound train pulling into Fifty-eighth Street. The locomotive is in reverse because it operated in either direction. In 1897, the South Side Elevated Railroad was formed to take over the bankrupt line. (Bruce Moffat collection.)

In 1895, Chicago's other "L"s began running with electric power, and the South Side Line was sure to follow suit. Here a crew installs cables at Fifty-eighth Street in 1897. Behind the workers, steam locomotive 30 pulls a southbound train out of the station. (Bruce Moffat collection.)

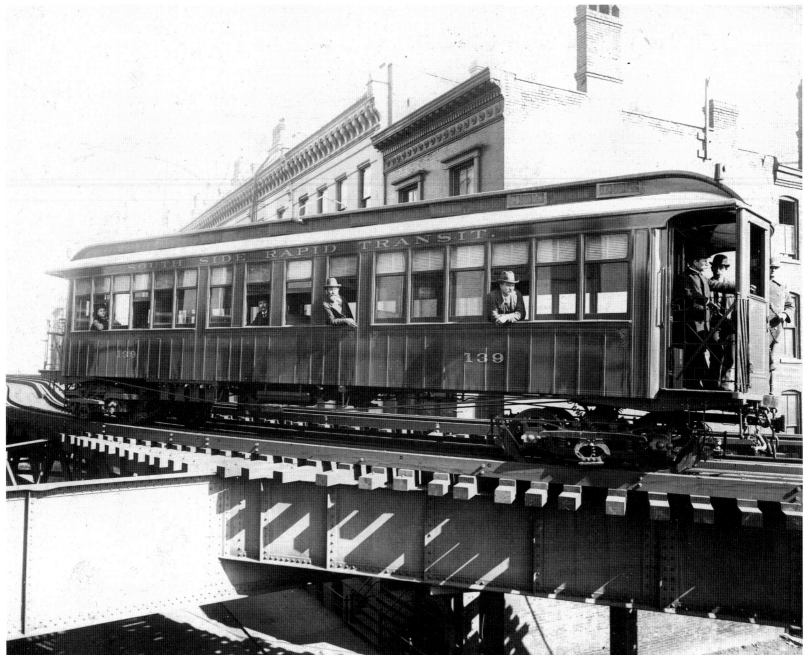

Coming later to electric power than the other "L's, the South Side Line was able to leapfrog them with multiple-unit train control, a new technology that allowed one operator to control several motorcars from any operating cab. Prior to this, each motorcar required its own operator, which limited most trains to one motorcar pulling a few trailers. The Manhattan elevated line rejected this new technology, so inventor Frank Sprague brought it to Chicago. Here he rides in the cab (on the right) during a test run past Harrison Street and Wabash Avenue in 1898. (CTA.)

As the South Side developed, ridership grew, creating demand for more transit. In 1903, the city allowed the "L" to construct a third track for express service above the public alley between Twelfth and Forty-third Streets. In exchange, the company had to pave the area below its track along that stretch and maintain it as public space. To open space under its tracks, the South Side "L" demolished 11 ground-level station houses north of Forty-third Street and replaced them with mezzanine-level stations, such as this one at Thirty-first Street. This, in turn, required the "L" to raise its structure at each new station, creating a gentle roller-coaster effect still visible. All the mezzanine stations were later demolished. (W. R. Keevil collection, photograph by C. E. Keevil.)

One way to build ridership, especially for weekends, was to serve entertainment venues, such as the Washington Park Race Track, visible on the right beyond the train running over Sixty-third Street west of Cottage Grove Avenue in about 1901. The cars are still identified as South Side Rapid Transit, even though the new South Side Elevated Railroad had taken over in 1897. (W. R. Keevil collection.)

The racetrack was popular, as seen in this 1900 photograph of "Derby Day." Clearly some of these racing fans in their finery at the Lawn Club House had not arrived on the "L." Still, most rode some form of rail transportation to the track—and everywhere else—during an era when rail controlled more than 95 percent of the transit market. (Chicago History Museum.)

When objections to gambling shut down the racetrack in 1904, the more family-oriented White City Amusement Park took its place nearby at Sixty-third Street and South Park Avenue (now King Drive). This view from the White City's airship in 1914 shows that the "L" stopped at the park's front gate. (CTA.)

An upper yard at Sixty-first Street and a lower yard at Sixty-third Street were built starting in 1893 on either side of where the "L" turns east. The two-block-long upper yard, one of the country's largest elevated railroad yards, is in the foreground of this 1964 view southeast. Today these yards are used to store materials and to store and maintain non-revenue vehicles. (CTA.)

The single-track stub terminal of the South Side "L" at Congress Street in the alley east of State Street was taken out of passenger service in 1949. Here in the 1950s, workers remove the tracks over Congress Street as part of a street-widening project. The Chicago North Shore and Milwaukee Railroad (North Shore) used the remainder of the terminal as a baggage facility until 1963, and then it was torn down. The Congress/Wabash station, just half a block east, may seem oddly close to the terminal, but it was built in 1897 when the South Side "L" gained access to the Loop "L," thereby diverting through trains from its stub terminal. Congress/Wabash was closed in 1949 and demolished in the 1950s, also for the street widening. (CTA.)

Opposite: Its initial franchise required the Lake Street "L" to run an experimental steam-powered monorail developed by Joe Meigs, seen here on a test track in Cambridge, Massachusetts, in 1886. Meigs's monorail was innovative, with its cylindrical body and raised cab. Imagine it riding above Lake Street today. Probably because the president of the new "L" was also president of the company that owned the monorail's marketing rights, the "L" spent more than $50,000 on licensing fees for the monorail before choosing traditional technology. (Joe Vincent Meigs Papers, Manuscripts and Archives, Yale University Library.)

THREE

SECOND "L"—LAKE STREET

The initial success of the South Side "L" encouraged businessmen to plan three additional lines, all of which were operating by 1900. The history of the second line, the Lake Street Elevated Railway, is rife with corruption, bribery, kickbacks, and financial chicanery. It was controlled by Michael McDonald, known as "King Mike," who was reputed to have made a fortune in gambling and vice. From there he diversified into transit—not so much to run trains but more to skim profits, manipulate stock,

and shake down potential competitors. He had considerable influence over politicians, from local aldermen to the governor.

The city council granted McDonald a franchise in 1888 to build an "L" above Lake Street, but potential investors found its requirements too restrictive. The franchise was good for only 25 years, would have prevented the line from crossing the Chicago River into downtown, and required fares to be lowered after two years from the customary 5¢ to 4¢. Lobbying the

city council and state legislature won a more favorable franchise in 1890, although construction had already begun the year before.

By 1892, McDonald had watered the company's stock to the point that debt had risen to $17 million while the company had less than $4 million in assets. He sold out to new owners, who raised additional capital, completed construction, and began operations in November 1893.

Workers raise the first columns of the Lake Street "L" at Lake Street and Milwaukee Avenue in 1889. Contract disputes, funding problems, political maneuvering, and a lawsuit from a competing streetcar company interrupted construction several times. (CTA, George Krambles collection.)

This cartoon depicts "King Mike" operating with "corruption tonic" and "bulldozing pills." Unknown is the identity of the person represented by the tiger that McDonald is spoon-feeding—a politician, a competitor, the public? (Chicago History Museum Library.)

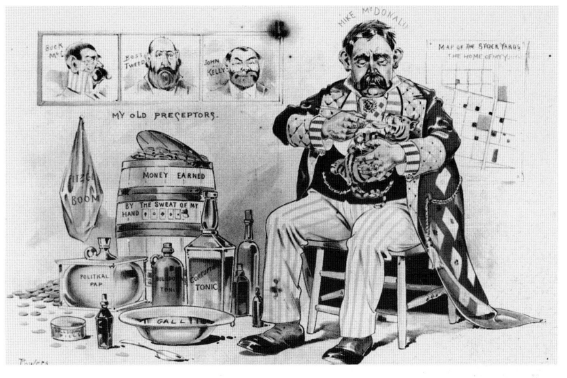

The new "L" was determined to build down the middle of Lake Street rather than along alleys. For this, the 1883 Adams Law required written consent from a majority of owners (measured in frontage feet) along each mile of street. This set the stage for selling—and rescinding—consent. This 1893 view looks east from west of Rockwell Street, about where the track structure narrows to save money on steel. (CTA.)

Access to the business district was contentious. Through intensive lobbying and undoubtedly some bribes, McDonald got permission to build downtown over Market Street (now Wacker Drive) from Lake Street south to a terminal at Madison Street. Opposition was weak there because Market Street was wide and full of factories. In this 1893 view, construction advances north from Madison Street. Revenue service finally began on November 6, 1893, north from the Madison stub terminal to Lake Street, then west to California Avenue. (CTA.)

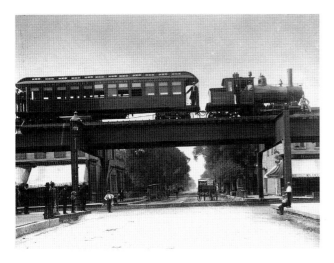

Clarence A., one of the 25 locomotives named after company officials or investors, pulls the first train of the Lake Street "L" across Oakley Boulevard. (Clarence A. Knight was the line's legal counsel.) Remarkably for the time, five locomotives were named after women. Meanwhile, engine 24 was named after corrupt McDonald. In 1894, Charles Tyson Yerkes saw that the Lake Street "L" was in trouble so he bought it for the bargain price of $1 million. (CTA.)

Unlike McDonald, Yerkes wanted to run trains and offer transit services rather than just make a fortune by bilking investors. This portrait of Yerkes, never before published, shows his resolve. In 1987, Susan Gamble Yerkes (Charles's great-granddaughter) gave the painting to Chicago attorney Michael Dorf, who had been working to rehabilitate Yerkes's reputation. He and Claudia Howard Queen wrote *Titans*, a musical about Yerkes. (Michael Dorf.)

Despite severe financial problems, the line gradually extended west, reaching Oak Park in 1899. Here a crew poses with unnamed engine 26 at Cicero Avenue in 1896. The line converted to electric power in 1896, buying its electricity from Charles Tyson Yerkes's extensive streetcar operations that generated their own power. (CTA.)

In 1899, the Lake Street "L" extended service to the Harlem Race Track. Local civic leaders tried to ignore the racetrack, but the large number of express trains filled with gamblers indicated that it was a popular destination—and prompted residents to complain that the "L" slighted them in favor of racing fans. (Bruce Moffat collection.)

By 1903, financial problems had caught up with the Lake Street "L" and the company went bankrupt. The Chicago and Oak Park Elevated Railroad (C&OP) took over in 1904. Here passengers ride on the longitudinal seats of a typical "bowling alley" car in 1909. Some people considered it risqué for unacquainted men and women to sit side by side in such an intimate, unchaperoned setting. Soon the C&OP bought the first group of "L" cars with reversible seats arranged crosswise of the car so everyone could ride facing forward. (Chicago History Museum.)

The Halsted station house displays the beautiful gingerbread styling and Queen Anne architecture typical of the original Lake Street "L" stations. The building shown here in 1946 was demolished in 1996, but a similar renovated one at Ashland with a pagoda-like tower is the oldest station house (1893) still in operation on the entire "L" system. (CTA, photograph by C. E. Keevil.)

Opposite: The Metropolitan "L" was so innovative that on April 27, 1895, *Scientific American* featured construction of the line on its cover. The four-track main line cut a broad swath through Chicago's West Side. (*Scientific American.*)

FOUR

THIRD "L"—METROPOLITAN

Compared with Lake Street, the Metropolitan West Side Elevated Railroad was well managed and efficiently operated. In 1892, it incorporated and received a city franchise. Construction began the following year and progressed rapidly. Operations began in 1895; almost immediately it became the city's largest "L" line.

Just like its two predecessor "L" lines (the South Side and Lake Street), the Met, as it was called, was to be powered by steam locomotives. Based on the success of the Columbian Intramural Railway during the World's Columbian Exposition, however, the Met decided to use the uncovered, trackside, third-rail electrical power system that had functioned so well at the fair. This made the Met the country's first permanent electrified elevated transit line.

Electrification was especially important at this time because Chicago's streetcars had begun to use electric power in 1890, allowing them to offer larger, more comfortable cars that were better heated and lighted than "L" cars. Subsequently the "L" and the streetcar would compete aggressively for passengers, with the streetcar usually prevailing.

To provide electricity, the Met built a massive power plant at Loomis Street in the middle of its main line. The smokestacks rose 150 feet. Fourteen coal-fired boilers could generate the equivalent of an astonishing 9,000 horsepower. The plant operated until 1914, when the Met started purchasing power from Commonwealth Edison. It was later demolished to make way for the Congress (now Eisenhower) Expressway. (CTA, George Krambles collection.)

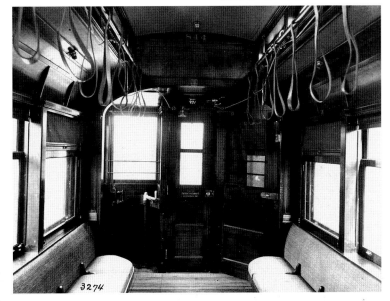

The line opened between Canal Street and Robey Street (now Damen Avenue) on May 6, 1895, with 55 motorized passenger cars and 100 trailers. Early "L" car interiors were sparse, as seen in this car built for the Met in 1904. (CTA.)

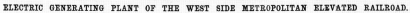
ELECTRIC GENERATING PLANT OF THE WEST SIDE METROPOLITAN ELEVATED RAILROAD.

Here is a look inside the Met's Loomis power plant, as depicted in the *Scientific American* article, which exclaimed, "It is needless to say that the operation of an elevated road by electricity represents the perfection of traction systems as far as passengers and dwellers on the line are concerned." (*Scientific American.*)

The four branches of the Met spread out like fingers across the West Side, splitting away from the main line at the Marshfield Junction, seen here looking east. First to open was the Logan Square Branch, which ran about five miles northwest from the Marshfield Junction to a terminal at Logan Square (below, photographed much later). In 1895, two more branches followed: Garfield Park, which ran four miles west from the junction to Forty-eighth Street (now Cicero Avenue), and Humboldt Park, which split off the Logan Square Branch near Robey Street (now Damen Avenue) and ran about two miles west to Lawndale Avenue. The Douglas Park Branch opened in 1896 and ran southwest about two and a half miles from the junction to Western Avenue. (CTA.)

Soon after the line opened, it began crossing the river over this bridge north of Van Buren Street to serve its Franklin Street terminal. Still, the terminal was only one block east of the river. This limited access to the heart of the city gave streetcars a decided advantage. Seen here around 1920, this innovative rolling lift bridge was a new design created to fit into a narrow space along the river between two swing bridges. Furthermore, it was composed of side-by-side spans, which allowed one span to handle all traffic if the other span needed to be repaired. The Met was the only "L" to ever own and operate a drawbridge. All other "L" river crossings are over city street bridges. (CTA.)

On December 23, 1895, the Met experienced what might have been the first major "L" mishap. In the midnight hours, a motorman apparently dozed off as his single motorcar ran off the end of the Garfield Park Branch. None of the three people on board were seriously injured, but it took two days to hoist the car back onto the tracks. Critics blamed the accident on electric operations, which left train control in the hands of only one person. (On steam locomotives, the fireman could intervene if the engineer became incapacitated.) Nonetheless, electric traction was here to stay. The innovative Met offered advanced services such as announcements of approaching trains. Here the Met's employee "Elevated Band" plays in the Laramie Avenue yard on the Garfield Park Branch in 1920. (Left, Bruce Moffat collection; below, Chicago History Museum.)

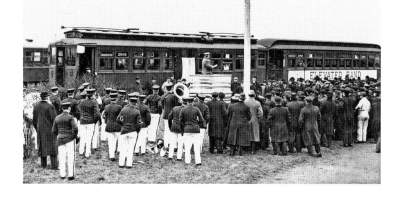

Since the Met did not initially reach the city center and its outlying tracks served sparsely populated areas, one reporter wrote in 1895 of the Douglas Park Branch, "it begins and ends nowhere." This changed as the "L" sparked development along its routes. A 1902 postcard promotes property along the "L" as land of opportunity. (Bruce Moffat collection.)

When the Met converted to multiple-unit train control in 1904, several motorcars could be operated efficiently in the same train, making longer trains possible. The line had periods of financial difficulties but typically rebounded. Three of its four branches were extended, sooner or later. Here a train approaches the Loop over the former Met main line around 1940. (CTA.)

When the Met began accessing the Loop "L" at Van Buren Street and Fifth Avenue (now Wells Street) in 1897, ridership quickly surpassed the limitations of the Loop structure. In 1904, this four-track stub terminal opened at Fifth Avenue just south of Jackson Street. By 1907, the Met was operating 114 rush-hour trains from this terminal, even though other trains continued accessing the Loop "L" via the Met's connection at the southwest corner of that structure just one-half block south at Van Buren Street and Fifth Avenue. Later the Chicago Aurora and Elgin (CA&E) interurban shared this terminal with the Met. This 1925 view east shows how the Insurance Exchange Building (occupying only half of its current footprint) loomed over the terminal, which was demolished in 1964. (CTA, George Krambles collection.)

Opposite: This 1920s map shows that the terminals of the four original "L's" were outside the central business district. The South Side "L" got no closer than Congress Street; the Lake Street "L" no closer than Market Street (now Wacker Drive); the Metropolitan "L" no closer than Fifth Avenue (now Wells Street); and the Northwestern "L" no closer than North Water Street (although its terminal was not built until 1908, well after the Loop "L" was completed). Main-line railroad stations were barred from the central district too. (Bruce Moffat collection.)

UNION LOOP "L"

Loved by some, reviled by others, the Loop "L" has defined downtown Chicago for more than a century. In fact, the Loop "L" gave the city center its name. From the beginning, each of the four original "L"s wanted the same access to the heart of the city that their rival streetcar lines had been granted. Nonetheless, concerns about noise, soot, safety, and (later) electricity caused business owners and politicians to deny "L" lines that access. It took the power and cunning of Charles Tyson Yerkes to bring the original "L" lines into the heart of Chicago, giving them a practical, common right-of-way to serve the needs of that

time—and of future generations.

Yerkes came to Chicago from Philadelphia in 1881 with a checkered background in finance and transit that included prison time. Primarily a financial wizard, he quickly established himself in the local banking elite. Yerkes began buying up horsecar railways on the North and West Sides, starting with the North Chicago City Railway, which he and his associates acquired in 1886 without spending a penny of their own money. He invested heavily to convert many of his horsecar lines, which were growing in number, to cable and electric power.

Soon Yerkes owned or controlled two-thirds of Chicago's street railways. Initially he tried to block elevated transit because it was so expensive to build and would pull riders from his street railways. He quickly realized, however, that elevated lines could not be stopped so he decided to control them rather than compete with them. From then on, he championed the "L" and a common, shared interchange (albeit at a cost to passengers of another nickel to transfer). This chapter tells how Yerkes built the Union Loop, a two-mile structure around one-quarter of a square mile of some of the country's most prized real estate.

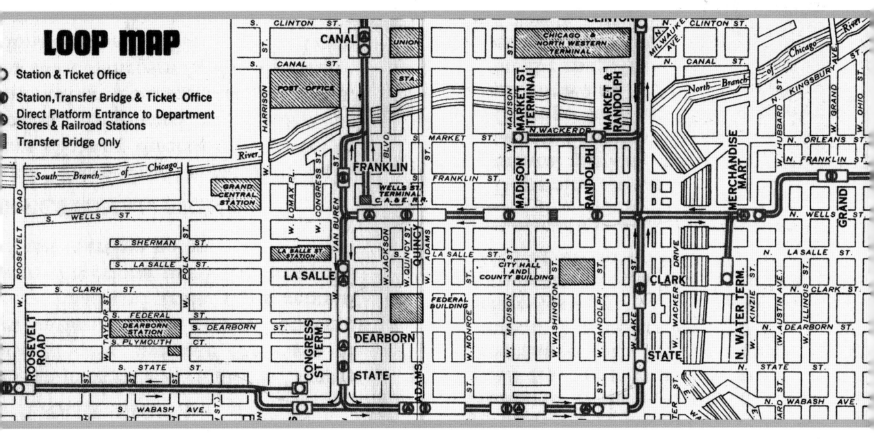

In 1893, the Lake Street "L" secured a franchise to build a downtown loop through the alleys on either side of Lake Street east to Wabash Avenue. Yerkes's Northwestern "L" also had a franchise for a proprietary downtown loop, and the two loops would have intersected in the alley between Lake and Randolph Streets, west of LaSalle Street. The first to build would save money by not having to cross over the other's tracks. On the night of June 7, 1894, the Lake Street "L" surreptitiously built a short structure there. The Northwestern "L" sued, but one month later Yerkes ended the dispute by covertly acquiring the Lake Street "L." This gave him more leverage to build his desired common Loop "L." He began by portraying its northern leg as a mere extension of his Lake Street "L." This view west on Lake Street at Wabash Avenue in 1895 shows workmen positioning the last columns of that "extension." (CTA.)

Yerkes finessed the second leg of the Loop "L," the western one over Fifth Avenue (now Wells Street), the same way—as just another extension, this time of his yet-to-be-built Northwestern "L." By now, property owners were on to him. In exchange for their consent, they extracted payoffs on average of $50 per foot of street frontage. For the third leg (the eastern one over Wabash Avenue, seen here looking north at Madison in 1908), Yerkes formed a new company, the Union Elevated Railway. It secured a franchise in 1895 but had to pay property owners along Wabash Avenue an average of $100 per foot of street frontage for their consent. (CTA.)

For the last leg, Yerkes outmaneuvered the remaining opposition to his Loop "L" by forming in 1896 another company, the Union Consolidated Elevated. It secured consent agreements to build over Van Buren Street between Wabash Avenue and Halsted Street, a distance of more than one mile. Yerkes intended to build less than half of this distance, but he knew that the factory owners on the western portion of the proposed line would give him the majority of consents he needed to build the last leg. This view looks west from the southeast corner of the Union Loop shortly after it was completed, with a train at the State and Van Buren platform. The Union "L" cost more than $1 million, but Yerkes did not go to all that expense just to serve the public. His Union Elevated Railway owned the new structure and was guaranteed $250,000 a year by the four "L" lines to use it. (Chicago History Museum.)

The first test run occurred on September 6, 1897, and service began on October 3 when a Lake Street "L" entered the Union Loop at Fifth Avenue (now Wells Street) where the train is positioned in this photograph (taken decades later) looking west. It took 25 minutes to circle the Loop, which included 12 stations and four sharp corners that limit speeds and cause congestion to this day. (CTA.)

WABASH AVE. AND ELEVATED RAILROAD, LOOKING NORTH FROM VAN BUREN ST.

All lines saw a significant increase in ridership from their new hard-fought access to the city center. Weekly ridership on the Metropolitan "L," for example, jumped from 40,000 to 60,000. Within a few months, trains cluttered the Loop "L." Within a few years, each track was handling up to 65 trains per hour. This postcard looks north on Wabash Avenue at Van Buren Street. (Lake County Illinois Discovery Museum, Curt Teich Postcard Archives.)

After the Loop "L" opened, the three original "L's closed their stub terminals. The Loop "L" quickly reached capacity, so the lines reactivated their terminals to stage trains and offer rush-hour service. This photograph of the Lake Street "L" terminal shows how this would have worked, although it was not taken until 1948, when the structure was being demolished. (CTA.)

Initially people viewed the "L" with suspicion, especially in the Loop where so many rode it and walked under the tracks. Would the trains fall off? Was the electricity dangerous? In 1908, a cop and bystanders observe where a man fell to the ground near Lake and Market (now Wacker Drive) Streets. Note the streetcar running under the "L" on Lake Street. (Chicago History Museum.)

With four independent "L's using the Loop—and no free transferring—each station on each side of the tracks was separated into two areas with their own entrances, fare booths, and platforms. A vestige of this can still be seen at many Loop "L" stations, including Quincy, seen here with an Evanston Special picking up passengers. Fare registers (inset) above the ticket booths were used to ring up fares to assure passengers that the agent did not pocket their money. These registers were left in place in 1988 when Quincy was restored to its 1897 condition. (CTA; inset, Greg Borzo.)

The Auditorium Building, Louis Sullivan's masterpiece, stands behind the Congress stub terminal as an excellent example of the many world-famous architectural treasures visible along the "L," especially downtown. Unusual views of beautiful and important buildings, parks, and historical sites abound. (CTA.)

Surprisingly the presence of the "L" has helped preserve some of Chicago's oldest buildings, including the Washington Block at 40 North Wells Street, seen here behind platform extension work in 1926. The "L" depressed property values along the streets it darkened, so this relic and others like it built shortly after the Great Chicago Fire of 1871 have never been replaced. (CTA.)

Most downtown stations had second-floor entrances from their platforms directly into department stores or train stations, as seen on both platforms in this stylish drawing from the cover of a Chicago transit map in the mid-1930s. Such direct entrances remained in use until the 1960s. The first one in 1900 linked the Madison/Wabash station with the Schlesinger and Mayer department store, later Carson Pirie Scott. The shuttered entrance can still be seen on that building (to the right of the picture window) looking west from the "L" platform. (Above, Bruce Moffat collection; below, Greg Borzo.)

This scene north from the northwest corner of the Union Loop shows a typical busy day in the early 1920s when this intersection handled up to 1,100 cars an hour, making it the world's busiest railroad crossing. At that time, trains ran around the Loop counterclockwise on both tracks. On the left, a South Side Englewood Express of wooden cars heads south; on the right, a Logan Square train of "baldie" steel cars also turns south; in the right background, a train of South Side wooden cars turns right, through-routed north. (CTA.)

Opposite: Charles Tyson Yerkes routed his Northwestern "L" well inland from his busy streetcar line on Clark Street. This 1897 view north at Willow Street shows columns and crossbeams laid out alongside the alley between Sheffield Avenue and Bissell Street for the construction of the new "L." North of about Belmont Avenue, Chicago was sparsely settled. Farmers there supplied vegetables and flowers to the growing city. (Krambles-Peterson Archive.)

SIX

FOURTH "L"—NORTHWESTERN

The last of the original "L" lines, the Northwestern Elevated Railroad, was incorporated in 1893. Even so, it did not begin operating until 1900 due to repeated financial, political, labor, and construction delays. Its story is the most colorful of the original "L's, in part because the controversial Charles Tyson Yerkes, its principal backer, was calling the shots.

In early 1894, Yerkes won a franchise from the city to build an "L" from downtown north to Wilson Avenue, with several branches and extensions along the way. Stiff penalties were to be assessed if the line did not meet certain standards and deadlines, including that service begin by January 1, 1897. The work would see a series of fits and starts and three extensions from the city before the line was finally up and running for good.

Despite his success building and running transit systems, Yerkes was reviled for shady business practices, bribery, and undue political influence. Shortly after completing the Northwestern "L," Yerkes was forced out of town by business competitors, political opponents, and angry riders who thought that the wealthy, powerful traction baron put his profits and dividends above their comfort and convenience. Yerkes moved to London, where he helped to build the London Underground transit system, and died in New York in 1905.

As a private entrepreneur, Charles Tyson Yerkes did not have the power of eminent domain. His Northwestern "L" had to zigzag its way through the North Side, finding the cheapest route with the least resistance from established businesses, churches, and residents. The resulting curves may not have presented operating problems in 1900, when a single motorized car typically hauled a few trailers, but the curves slow down trains today. North Avenue parallels the "L" on the right and intersects the curve. Clybourn Avenue parallels the "L" on the left, as the structure continues north. Construction of the Northwestern "L" began in 1896 near Fullerton Avenue. Soon thereafter, the work was halted by lack of funds due to a nationwide economic downturn. The directors almost abandoned the project, but Yerkes raised more money and work resumed. Construction stopped again in 1897 due to additional financial difficulties. (CTA.)

After yet another break, construction resumed in 1899 with new financing. But if the "L" failed to begin operating by January 1, 1900, it would forfeit $100,000 to the city. The Northwestern "L" rushed hard-to-get supplies to its construction sites and hired extra workers. By December 30, 1899, only one track and three stations had been completed. Nevertheless, the line sent a train downtown in a desperate bid to demonstrate that it had met its deadline. This photograph taken a few months later does not show that first train but a similar one southbound at the point where the Northwestern "L" joins the Loop at Lake and Wells Streets. (CTA.)

Unsafe operating conditions and unfinished work caused the city to declare the company's franchise expired and order service to cease. This view west at the Sedgwick station site taken on January 25, 1900, shows that much work was, indeed, unfinished—even weeks later. (CTA.)

Undaunted, Charles Tyson Yerkes sent out another train on January 1, 1900. Police boarded it and arrested the crew, but one passenger was a company official. He grabbed the controls and headed downtown, taking the same path as this train passing the still unfinished Chicago station later that year. Fifty police officers gathered on the tracks of the Union Loop, but they scattered when the train did not slow down. (CTA.)

Next the police placed railroad ties across the tracks to block the train's return north after it circled the Loop. The runaway "L" outwitted the police, again, by turning west onto the tracks of the Lake Street "L." Eventually the most notorious run in "L" history was halted at the stub terminal of the Lake Street "L." Lawyers smoothed out the problems caused by Yerkes's defiance and even coaxed another extension out of the city, this time until May 31, 1900. That launch went well. Here a southbound train passes the Kinzie station (still under construction) toward the Loop in June 1900. (CTA.)

In 1908, the Northwestern "L" built something the other original "L's already had: a downtown stub terminal for extra rush-hour capacity. It was located along North Water Street (now Carroll Avenue) between Clark and Wells Streets. This view of the terminal at Clark shows company employees at the foot of some pretty formidable stairs (marked with advertisements). Note the dining car staff member on the North Shore interurban train in the upper left. (CTA.)

The first Wells Street bridge was a swing model pivoting on its center pier. Because the pier blocked the river's increasingly large boats, the bridge was replaced in 1921 by a double-deck bascule lift structure. The old bridge operated until the new one was built in this upright position. Once the new bridge was nearly completed, the old one was demolished so the new one could be lowered. (Krambles-Peterson Archive, photograph by A. W. Johnson.)

Originally the Northwestern "L" went only as far north as Wilson (seen here in 1917), but that did not remain the terminus for long. (CTA.)

This 1900 photograph shows the four-track structure north of the Chicago station. Charles Tyson Yerkes wanted four tracks along the entire line but had to settle for two tracks south of Chicago in exchange for the city's permission to build over downtown streets. The long platform at the Chicago station allowed two trains to berth simultaneously as they moved through this bottleneck. (CTA.)

All four tracks from this point near Armitage (seen here in the mid-1940s) north to Howard are still in use. In the other direction, from here south to Chicago, the outside pair of tracks was abandoned after the North Shore interurban stopped operating in 1963. Long sections of these abandoned tracks between Armitage and Chicago can still be seen. (Krambles-Peterson Archive.)

In 1908, the "L" extended service to Howard and beyond to Evanston at ground level. In 1914–1922 it elevated the track from Wilson to Howard on an embankment rather than a steel structure. This was done to support the weight of freight cars that the "L" handled from 1920 to 1973 between Church Street in Evanston and Irving Park Road in Chicago. A huge yard was built at Wilson in 1900. Much later, a massive four-track repair and maintenance building, seen in the center background of this view south in 1961, was added. A continuous four-track main line had just been completed here, replacing a two-track bottleneck. (CTA.)

Opposite: The South Side "L" added four branches in just a few years. One going southwest three miles from Fifty-ninth Street to Englewood was incorporated in 1903 and built in stages, with service beginning in 1905. This view looks northeast along the Englewood Branch from a roof at Sixty-third Street and Harvard Avenue in 1924. (CTA.)

SEVEN

EXPANSION AND UNIFICATION

No sooner had each "L" been constructed than each began to expand. They extended main lines, built branches, partnered with interurban railroads, added more and longer trains, and launched express and other services. This process, albeit marked by occasional retrenchments, continues to this day. This chapter cannot look at each expansion or new branch, but it will touch on a few significant and colorful ones.

It will also look at the most important change in the "L" during the first decades of the 20th century: unification of the disparate lines into one comprehensive system. From the beginning, "L" passengers were hampered by the lack of crosstown service. And while the mandated 5¢ fare (which lasted from 1892 to 1918) was reasonable, patrons complained that they had to shell out another nickel every time they transferred along their trip.

Charles Tyson Yerkes with his Loop "L" had achieved a measure of unification, but the person most responsible for full integration of lines and services was utilities magnate Samuel Insull. He launched his impressive career working for Thomas Edison, and many people considered him a genius. Ultimately Insull built an empire of electricity generating plants and distribution networks in 32 states with some $2.5 billion in assets. His interest in generating electricity overlapped nicely with running transit companies, which would become major customers of his power plants.

In 1907, the Englewood Branch sprouted its own offshoot, the Normal Park Branch. It had only four stations and ran 0.9 miles south from Harvard to Sixty-ninth Street, between Normal and Parnell Avenues. Two additional branches of the South Side "L" extended east and west from Indiana, seen here looking west in 1910. The 1.2-mile Kenwood Branch going east opened in 1907 over the tracks in the lower left corner. The three-mile Stock Yards Branch opened in 1908 and terminated on the stub track in the center. The main "L" curves off to the left, where a long express train is passing. (CTA.)

This view north around 1915 shows the Kenwood Branch terminal at Forty-second Place and Oakenwald Avenue, complete with an attractive redbrick Greek Revival station house. The line competed with streetcars and Illinois Central local trains in the densely populated, relatively affluent area. (CTA, George Krambles collection.)

The most colorful (and odoriferous) branch went through the stockyards carrying workers to packinghouses—as well as tourists to see the slaughtering and dine at fine restaurants in the vicinity. It had seven stations with names like Armour and Swift. The unusual bow trolley on the top of these cars, seen near Halsted in 1911, was needed to move cars around yards not equipped with a third rail. (CTA.)

Unification of the four original "L" lines came slowly and gradually. Samuel Insull saw them as large potential utility customers but quickly realized that unification of the lines could cut operating costs and streamline services. Soon he was at the helm. After much negotiating and maneuvering, Insull and his partners formed the Chicago Elevated Railways Collateral Trust (CER) in 1911. Under the outstanding direction of Britton Budd, CER ran the four "L's as one company, although each line maintained its own identity. In 1913, CER's first major action (prompted by a city ordinance) was the through, cross-town routing of trains and free transfers between "L" lines. This view north at Stony Island Avenue and Sixty-third Street shows signs advertising the new policy. The several streetcar companies then operating had recently instituted similar changes. (Bruce Moffat collection.)

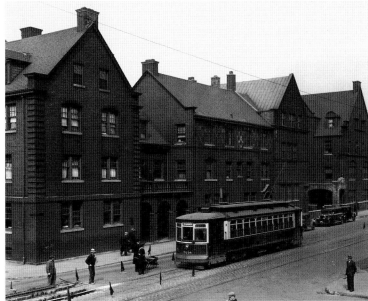

Despite its rapid growth, the "L" still played second fiddle to the ubiquitous streetcar, such as this one in front of Hull House on Halsted Street. In 1906, the "L" carried 132 million riders and streetcars carried 402 million; in 1916, the ratio was 181 million to 686 million. Reaching all populated parts of Chicago, streetcars did a good job linking people and neighborhoods across a democratic, gridlike street layout. (CTA.)

To handle the surge generated by the universal transfer, CER ordered 128 new 4000-series cars, nicknamed "baldies" because their roofs had no ventilators, roof boards, or trolley poles. More important, they were the first steel-bodied cars. A subsequent order included new passenger comforts such as luxurious interiors, fans, shades, and cushioned seats, as seen here in the 1920s. These cars were nicknamed "plushies." (CTA.)

In 1924, Samuel Insull combined the four "L" lines into the Chicago Rapid Transit Company (CRT). CRT consolidated control of electric substations scattered across the system at a traction power supervisor's office in the Edison building, CRT's main office location, seen here in 1926. That year, the "L" carried an all-time high 229 million passengers over 227 track miles, with about 5,000 weekday trains. (CTA.)

Some say the "L" had its best days under CRT, despite 23 years without any new cars. Ridership spiked in June 1926 due to the 28th International Eucharistic Congress, a worldwide Roman Catholic pilgrimage. Here riders at the Adams/Wabash station seek tickets on through service to Mundelein, where many congress events were held. Note the direct entrance from the "L" platform to the second floor of the building on the left. (Krambles-Peterson Archive.)

Based on strong ridership in 1924–1925, CRT began extensive improvements. From 1925 to 1931, it lengthened 112 platforms, including this one at Washington/Wells in 1926, to accommodate eight-car trains. It also rebuilt the Wells Street Terminal in 1927, covering it with a handsome three-story terra-cotta facade, and rebuilt the Logan Square terminal in 1928. (CTA.)

CRT also built a station at the Merchandise Mart, still under construction when this photograph looking north was taken in 1930. The covered platform on the right goes to the stub terminal over North Water Street (now Carroll Avenue) that the old Northwestern "L" had built. (CTA.)

The Depression hit the "L" hard. Ridership fell 8 percent in 1930 and a whopping 17 percent in 1931, when CRT posted its first loss ever, $1.5 million. Samuel Insull relinquished control in 1932 as CRT went into receivership. Subsequently he lost everything, including his beautiful Civic Opera Building pictured here behind the Lake Street "L" stub terminal on Market Street (now Wacker Drive) in 1930. The end of the Depression would not pull CRT out of financial trouble, primarily because of the loss of riders to automobiles. Other U.S. cities with rapid transit (Boston, New York, and Philadelphia) already had partial public agency participation by the 1920s. In Chicago, the stage was set for a government takeover of the "L," but other priorities, including World War II, delayed that until 1945. (CTA.)

Opposite: The close link between the "L" and suburban development is seen in this 1910 photograph of an excursion to Villa Park organized for potential home buyers by the real estate firm Ballard, Pottinger and Company. The chartered "L" cars ran over Aurora Elgin and Chicago Railway (a Chicago Aurora and Elgin predecessor) tracks. On other occasions, "L" cars carried picnic excursions as far as Aurora and Batavia. (Villa Park Historical Society.)

EIGHT

SERVING AND SHAPING THE SUBURBS

The "L" was always intended to reach the city limits, and beyond. The South Side "L" initially talked about running all the way to the Indiana border, and the Lake Street "L" planned to run as far west as Maywood. And working with the interurbans, the "L" extended its reach farther than it could have on its own.

The relationship between the "L" and the suburbs has not always been amicable, a pattern that continues to this day. There have been fights over fares, rights-of-way, service levels, franchise commitments, safety, and so on. For example, when Cicero required the Lake Street "L" to provide flagmen at grade crossings in 1899, the "L" suspended service rather than incur the cost. In 1902, Oak Park fought with the "L" about storing cars in the middle of Randolph Street. And many suburbs resisted the "L" because it brought two-flats and apartment buildings into areas that had been dominated by single-family homes.

Despite such disputes, the "L" helped the metropolitan area to grow and flourish by providing a vital, affordable link between the city and outlying areas. Today it reaches seven suburbs: Cicero, Evanston, Forest Park, Oak Park, Rosemont, Skokie, and Wilmette. In addition, it once entered Berwyn, Maywood, Bellwood, and Westchester. This chapter looks briefly at some of the ways the "L" not only provided transportation services to the suburbs but also helped to define their character.

Most suburban "L's operated at street level because building on the ground cost less than building up. This 1923 view north on Elmwood Avenue in Berwyn along the Douglas Park Branch shows two-flats rising near the "L," whose presence typically spurred home building, especially multifamily units. (CTA.)

When the Northwestern "L" extended service to Evanston in 1908, it used Chicago Milwaukee and St. Paul Railway (CM&StP) tracks. This view northeast at the Isabella station shows Evanston's limited development in 1928. Elsewhere in this suburb, the "L" competed with streetcars. (CTA.)

The "L" did not reach Wilmette until 1912, partly because residents feared it would generate construction of large apartment buildings. So the Northwestern "L" constructed a station platform under the cover of darkness and inaugurated service without permission. Legal challenges failed to shut down the extension. The Linden Avenue station (photographed in 1960) was built in 1913. (CTA.)

The Garfield Park Branch shared track and passengers with CA&E. Here a westbound CA&E freight passes Oak Park in 1935. The "L" and freight trains used the same gauge (56.5 inches), but freight cars were too wide for stations. Therefore the head brakeman used a hook to lift hinged boards along platforms as the train approached. The rear brakeman replaced the boards as the train passed. (CTA, photograph by Louis Sokol.)

CRT also worked closely with the North Shore interurban, which had gained access to downtown Chicago in 1919 over "L" tracks. For most of the years this interurban operated into Chicago, its southern terminus was Roosevelt, but from 1922 to 1938 it ran some trains as far south as Jackson Park. Cooperation between CRT, North Shore, and CA&E during the 1920s came naturally, in part because Samuel Insull controlled all three. This 1942 scene shows a North Shore train turning south at the southeast corner of the Loop "L," where Tower 12 (behind the train) was used to oversee traffic. (W. R. Keevil collection, photograph by C. E. Keevil.)

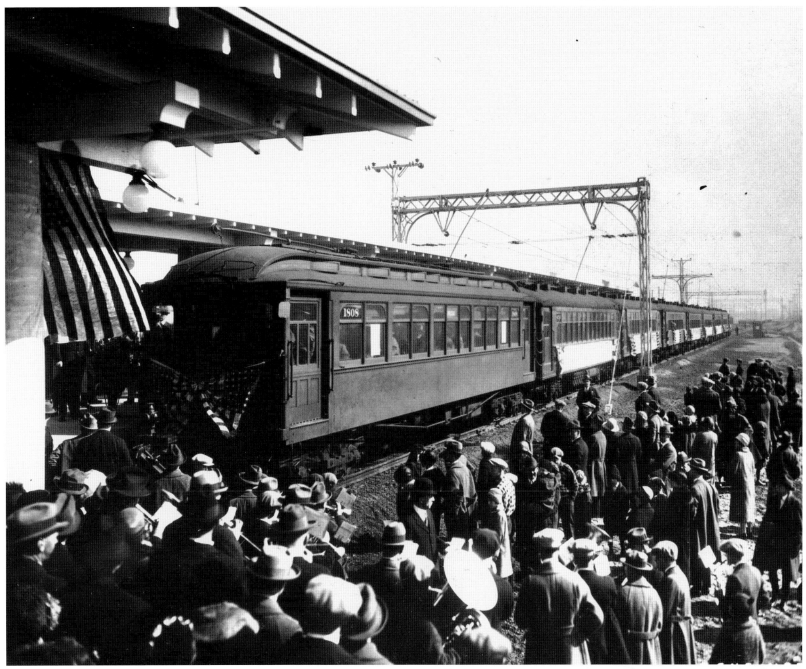

With this 1925 dedication, CRT launched a five-mile line to Niles Center (now Skokie). Promoters hoped it would stimulate housing along the largely uninhabited route. Insull, a master of promotion and advertising, hoped it would generate demand for electricity. A popular song urged home buyers to "follow Sam Insull's tip, take an "L" or auto trip, and pick out your Niles Center home." (CTA.)

CRT raised several suburban tracks to improve safety and operations. These 1928 photographs show the elevation of tracks between University Place and Isabella Street in Evanston that eliminated 13 grade crossings. CM&StP, the tracks' owner, built a temporary wood trestle (looking southwest toward Church Street) for northbound trains. For months, northbound and southbound trains operated on two different levels using double-deck stations at Foster, Noyes, and Central (the latter of which is below). The trestle was eventually filled in by an earthen embankment. Note the double set of rails on the track on the right. The outside set (first and third rails, from the left) is a "gauntlet" that allowed freight trains to clear platforms. No longer found on the "L," gauntlets should not be confused with guard rails—extra rails inside tracks to prevent a derailed train from going further off course. (CTA, George Krambles collection.)

In 1926, CRT and CA&E extended "L" service beyond the end of the Garfield Park Branch to Bellwood Avenue, then south to Roosevelt Road in Westchester. Four years later, service was extended further south and west to Twenty-second Street and Mannheim Road pictured here in 1930. Extremely low ridership on this remote branch led to its closing in 1951. (CTA.)

The Laramie Avenue station opened in 1910 when the Metropolitan "L" extended service to Cicero. It was well patronized when this photograph was taken in 1959. By 1980, however, ridership had fallen after a decline of industry in the area. The station was closed in 1992, but the station house has been preserved as one of the last remaining examples of its type. (CTA.)

When work began on the Congress (now Eisenhower) Expressway in the 1950s, the Garfield Park Branch temporarily rerouted alongside the construction and reduced service. CA&E trains no longer ran downtown to the Wells Street Terminal on "L" tracks. This 1953 view shows where the interurban connected with the "L" branch's terminal at Des Plaines Avenue in Forest Park. (CTA.)

A good candidate for elevation was the western end of the Lake Street "L," seen running on the street alongside the Chicago and North Western's embankment in this 1954 view west toward Central Avenue. Automobiles using the underpasses were vulnerable to collisions with ground-level trains, so in 1962 the "L" was relocated onto the embankment. (CTA.)

Looking west from Laramie in 1962 shows where the Lake Street "L" formerly descended to ground level (center left), as well as the new structure that would carry it, instead, onto the Chicago and North Western embankment (center right). Sharing a main-line railroad right-of-way affords today's West Side Green Line riders the unusual opportunity of riding beside commuter and freight trains, including doublestack container trains. (CTA.)

Mayor Richard J. Daley simulates destruction of a no-longer-needed crossing gate in October 1962 at a ceremony for the elevation of the Lake Street "L." Despite Daley's none-too-subtle endorsement, Sidney Yates lost this U.S. Senate race. The "L" has always been embroiled in Chicago-style politics, from patronage to cronyism. (CTA.)

On January 21, 1963, the storied North Shore stopped running on the "L" when it discontinued its Chicago–Milwaukee service. This photograph shows one of the interurban's final runs, a southbound "Silverliner" unloading two passengers at a Belmont platform reserved exclusively for the North Shore. (CTA.)

Mrs. Phillip Podulka of Glenview poses with Bernice T. Van der Vries, the first female Chicago Transit Authority (CTA) board member, showing geraniums that the Lake Shore Garden Club of Evanston had planted along the platform at the Davis station in 1965. (CTA.)

In 1948, CTA converted the Niles Center (now Skokie) service to a bus line, but in 1964 it reinstated the "L" service as the Skokie Swift. The project was accomplished with a grant from the federal government, which had just begun supporting urban transit. Initially CTA assigned experimental high-speed single cars with one-person crews (right). Ridership was five times higher than expected, so CTA quickly added high-capacity articulated cars. These cars had to convert from overhead to third-rail power at speed until 2004, when third rail was extended across the entire line. Known today as the Yellow Line, this service runs nonstop five miles between Howard and Dempster Streets, but intermediate stops are being considered. (CTA.)

The first maintenance and repair facilities of the "L" were at the edge of the city, including shops at Wilson Avenue, Sixty-first Street, Hamlin Boulevard, and Throop Street. As the city grew, some of these shops closed. In 1926, CRT built a paint shop in Skokie at a site that would become the 11-building complex shown here in 1964. Today Skokie Shops handles all heavy repairs for "L" cars; smaller facilities at the end of nearly every line conduct inspections and light maintenance. (CTA.)

Opposite: The earliest known use of a tunnel for urban mass transit in the United States was under the Chicago River in 1886 when Charles Tyson Yerkes acquired access to this tunnel at LaSalle Street that the city had built in 1871 to alleviate chronic delays crossing the river on bridges. With its steep grades and rank atmosphere, the tunnel was not useful, but Yerkes ran cable cars through it (seen here looking north from Randolph Street in 1906). He also ran cable through a tunnel under the river at Washington Street and a third one he built at Van Buren Street. His successors converted all three for electric trolleys. (CTA.)

NINE

FINALLY A SUBWAY

Subways are integral parts of the "L," even though that may sound like an oxymoron. Connecting several elevated portions of "L" lines around the city, the subways were built long after the "L" was developed. As a result, the term "L" refers to elevated and subway trackage (as well as surface trackage). In fact, of the 105 route miles of the "L," 38 run on elevated steel structures; 28 on highway medians; 21 on embankments; 11 through subways, and 7 at ground level.

The world's first subway was built in London in 1863; the first one in the United States was built in Boston in 1897. Chicago was slow to adopt the idea, largely due to its huge investment in surface and elevated lines.

Nonetheless, crushing traffic congestion downtown motivated politicians and the public to propose scores of subway plans. Bion Arnold suggested a comprehensive system in 1902; Daniel Burnham's Chicago Plan of 1909 called for burying the streetcar lines; and Mayor Carter Harrison Jr. advocated $133 million in 1913 to replace the Loop with a subway. All the while, funds to build a subway were accumulating. Starting in 1907, street railways paid into a traction fund to enable the city to eventually buy them out. The scheme yielded $40 million, which the city ultimately used to pay its share of the construction costs of the first two subways.

Many subway proposals were discussed for decades before Chicago finally built a line. This proposal, displayed at the Palmer House in the mid-1920s, used several "L" cars made by the new Buddy L toy company. Momentum and public support for a subway grew, but no progress was made until the New Deal offered incentives for public works. In 1937, the city applied for Works Progress Administration funds to build two subways, one under State Street and the other under Dearborn Street. Funds were granted, and officials broke ground on December 17, 1938, at State Street just south of Chicago Avenue. (CTA.)

Chicago's muddy soil limited the use of "cut-and-cover" techniques used to build subways in other cities. Instead two boring shields attacked the mud, each weighing 225 tons and measuring 25 feet in diameter. Outside the Loop, where soil was relatively firm, the mud was sliced or hacked away by men in the shields using heavy curved knives and power tools, as seen in this 1939 view. Three shifts of 20–30 men working on three levels could advance 25 feet per day. The soil's water content was as high as 58 percent, so compressed air was used to keep back the mud. Workers and materials had to pass through air locks at each shield entrance to prevent the compressed air from escaping. (CTA, George Krambles collection.)

Engineers approached tunnel construction under the river differently. At State Street, a clamshell dredge dug a deep trench across the river. Later, workers sank a prefabricated pair of 200-foot-long steel and concrete tubes into the trench. Made at a South Chicago dry dock, the subway tubes were floated 18 miles along two rivers and Lake Michigan to the construction site, a voyage that took about six hours. After the tubes were sunk into the trench, cofferdams were used to connect both ends of the tubes with the tunnels on either side of the river. (Krambles-Peterson Archive.)

Workers removed buildings, excavated streets, and relocated streetcar tracks near North and Clybourn Avenues. On the pedestrian's right, a track for the Clybourn streetcar rests on a wooden trestle above the State Street subway excavation. The subway will emerge in the middle of the preexisting "L" structure, where two trains pass overhead in the center of the photograph. (CTA.)

Workers build the mezzanine and stairways of the Dearborn Street subway's Madison-Monroe station in 1941. The Public Works Administration sign attests to the fact that Chicago owes its two original subways to the Great Depression. Note Mayor Edward Kelly's attempt to take credit for the project by putting his name on the other sign (left), as well as the sign in the photograph on the following page. (CTA.)

Deemed essential to the war effort, the 4.9-mile State Street subway was completed quickly. Here third rail is delivered in 1942. As World War II progressed, such materials became increasingly scarce. (CTA.)

Rail is installed in the State Street subway, but shortages left its walls and ceiling bare. The Dearborn Street subway fared worse. Lack of critical materials and manpower halted its construction in 1942. (CTA.)

City and federal officials and CRT personnel pose for the State Street subway's first inspection trip in April 1943. Afterward, Mayor Edward Kelly hams it up for the cameras proclaiming, "This is the most significant event in Chicago history." Nevertheless, the line did not begin operating until October 16, six months later. Chicago celebrated with fanfare, joining Boston, New York, and Philadelphia as the only U.S. cities with major subways. At first, CRT could not afford the streamlined subway cars it had planned to purchase, so 4000-series "baldie" and "plushie" cars were used, even though some were 30 years old. There were only 455 of these steel-bodied cars (required in the subway for fire safety), so service was restricted. With the arrival of more steel cars in the 1950s, the subway became extremely busy: up to one train every 90 seconds. (CTA.)

These 1943 shots put a happy face on tough times. The first one might have been intended to show that the State Street subway warranted its status as "critical" to the war because it transported soldiers and sailors. In any event, men and women in uniform rode for free. The second photograph harkens back to a time when public lockers were considered safe, the "L" provided restrooms and public telephones were ubiquitous. These "soundproof" telephone booths are so effective, according to publicity materials, "that privacy is assured without the use of doors." Even more impressive was the State Street subway's continuous 3,500-foot-long platform, the longest train platform in the world. Meanwhile, CRT noted it was lucky to have acquired reversible escalators "before Pearl Harbor since this equipment is virtually unobtainable during our present wartime economy." (CTA.)

A patron at Quincy on the Loop "L" reads a wartime poster exhorting Chicagoans to ride the "L," day or night. "Every needless mile makes our enemies smile," the poster says. "Our fighting forces *must* have all available crude rubber." (At that time, rubber was scarcer than petroleum; gas rationing was aimed at saving tires.) (CTA.)

Work on the Dearborn Street subway did not resume until late 1945, and then it progressed slowly. Here hand-operated cranes ease a third rail into position. CTA, created in 1945, inherited responsibility for finishing the Dearborn Street subway. (CTA.)

The diamond crossover at LaSalle in the Dearborn Street subway was nearly completed in 1950. It would switch southbound trains to the northbound track because this station served as the subway's southern terminus for seven years. This explains why its platforms and mezzanine are slightly larger than other downtown stations. (CTA.)

The Dearborn Street subway finally opened in February 1951, but only as far south as the LaSalle station at Congress Street. Mayor Martin Kennelly cuts the ribbon, joined by radio and movie celebrity Monte Blue in his trademark cowboy outfit. The tunnel boring shields were left in place, waiting for funds to complete the subway westward. (CTA.)

Not until 1958 was the full 3.8-mile Dearborn Street subway completed and connected with the new "L" running down the median of the Congress (now Eisenhower) Expressway that replaced the Garfield Park Branch "L," which was dismantled. Chicago's subways are considered part of the "L," as seen on this sign touting "FAST 'L'-Subway Trains!" In New York, where subways dominate mass transit, many locals speak of the "subway" even when they are on an elevated train. In Chicago, the opposite is true. Note that the subway is identified as an air raid shelter in this 1957 cold war scene looking north at State and Lake Streets. (CTA.)

Opposite: CTA inherited a system plagued by old equipment, low ridership, overused infrastructure, inefficient services, overlapping routes, and growing competition from automobiles. It streamlined operations by closing many stations and branches. The station at Fifty-first Street, seen here in 1946, escaped being closed, but this station house has since been replaced. (CTA.)

TEN

CHICAGO TRANSIT AUTHORITY

By the end of World War II, the "L" was on the brink of disaster. Bankrupted by the steep drop in ridership during the Depression, the system deferred critical maintenance. Then soaring ridership during the war, coupled with shortages, wore out much of the aging structure and obsolete equipment. Public ownership, an idea bandied about for half a century, became the only way to save the "L."

On April 12, 1945, the Illinois legislature created CTA as a municipal corporation to acquire, operate, and unify all modes of local transit. At the same time, the Chicago City Council granted CTA exclusive rights to operate such a system. Voters ratified both acts, six to one, on June 4, 1945. The laws gave CTA the power of eminent domain but no government support or taxing authority. Instead CTA was allowed to sell bonds that were to be repaid exclusively through the fare box. It was not until October 11, 1947, that CTA had sold enough bonds to buy Chicago Rapid Transit (the "L") for $12 million and Chicago Surface Lines (streetcars) for $75 million. In 1952, it bought Chicago Motor Coach (buses) for $16 million.

Thus, a system that under private ownership had repeatedly failed to generate sufficient revenue to meet operating needs was relaunched with the expectation it would pay its own way. CTA did just that, at least until the early 1970s.

In 1943–1948, the "L" had 227 stations, the most ever. Some were superfluous: imposed by local politicians; in areas ravaged by urban decay; or in undeveloped areas. Many were only one-quarter mile apart in an attempt to serve neighborhoods almost as closely as did streetcars, with stops one-eighth mile apart. Competition encouraged this practice until both surface and elevated systems were merged into CTA. One of CTA's first steps was to close lightly patronized lines and stations, including the Normal Park Branch, whose Sixty-ninth Street terminal is seen in this 1946 photograph. Over the ensuing years, CTA closed six branches and 99 stations. This relieved pressure on the aged fleet. In 1947, 745 of 1,200 cars were wooden, some of them built in the 1890s. The newest cars were already more than 20 years old. (W. R. Keevil collection, photograph by C. E. Keevil.)

Thirty experimental aluminum cars had been ordered in 1944, but war scarcities delayed their construction. Ultimately only four were built in 1947–1948. Each large articulated (jointed) car had three bodies, one of which the St. Louis Car Company builds here. Foregoing the experimental car, CTA ordered a more traditional design (the 6000-series below), the first of which was delivered in 1950. Two such cars arrive at the Skokie Shops via railroad flatcars in 1954. Their brisk acceleration and braking performance cut travel times by 10 percent. CTA purchased 770 similar cars, more than any other type, so some call this the quintessential "L" car. (CTA.)

The signal and control systems that CTA inherited were in no better condition than the aged fleet. At a time when automatic signals were the industry norm, most "L" trains (except those in the subway) ran "on sight." Motormen decided when and how fast to proceed—although they were guided by posted speed limits, signals, and spacing boards indicating safe following distances. Here a trackman holds a wrench used for tightening bolts at rail joints. Towermen would throw switches controlled by compressed air. (CTA.)

CTA purchased all modes of transit to integrate disparate services and eliminate wasteful competition. For instance, many streetcar lines ran parallel to—or even directly under—"L" lines, as seen in this view west at Hamlin along the Lake Street "L" in the early 1940s. CTA eventually replaced streetcars with buses and realigned some bus routes to feed riders onto the "L." (CTA.)

In 1948–1951, CTA introduced A/B skip-stop service on most lines. Little-used stations were designated A or B; busy stations were designated A/B. During most service hours, A trains stopped only at A or A/B stations; similarly for B trains. This sped up service considerably, although it increased waits at some little-used stations. Here a northbound A train to Howard picks up passengers at Indiana in 1955. (CTA.)

Upgrading stations took a lower priority. This view shows the interior of the Kedzie station on the Lake Street "L" in 1946. Although such coal stoves afforded little protection from Chicago's infamous winters, they were used until the 1970s. In most stations, electricity came from the third rail, so the lights would dim when a train accelerated. (W. R. Keevil collection, photograph by C. E. Keevil.)

Initially "L" operations required a conductor or guard between every two cars to control the doors. In the early 1950s, new "L" cars allowed all doors on a train to be operated from one place. This eliminated a lot of relatively dangerous—sometimes bitterly cold—jobs, like this one on the Lake Street "L" held in 1948 by Alastair Cameron Walker. It also permitted two-person crews. (CTA.)

Train controls and track signals evolved over the first 100 years of the "L"—and continue to evolve. In the late 1940s, CTA developed a line supervision control system and rolled it out systemwide by 1954. It used punch tapes (right) to authorize train departures from terminals and certain points along the route. Progress was tracked by train detectors along each line and registered on recorders like those to the left of the line supervisor (below) in the Merchandise Mart in 1958. "Fast, ultra-modern, two-way communication systems" allowed supervisors to speak with towermen and train operators, who could call in from trackside telephones. In these days before on-train telephones or radios, CTA claimed its system provided "more accurately dispatched and closely supervised" trains than any other system in the country. (CTA.)

Early on, CTA began to consolidate heavy maintenance work, traditionally performed all over the system, at its Skokie Shops. It moved machinery, transferred personnel, built facilities, and acquired new equipment. This drop table, added in 1956, allowed wheel assemblies to be replaced quickly. Also, a 45-ton wheel-truing machine allowed workers to reprofile wheels without removing them from cars. (CTA.)

Most of the branches CTA abandoned had low ridership, but the Humboldt Park Branch from Damen to Lawndale Avenues paralleling North Avenue enjoyed moderate patronage. Yet CTA downgraded the service and then replaced the short branch with limited bus service. It closed the branch in 1952 and dismantled the line soon thereafter. (CTA.)

Also in the early 1950s, CTA had to reconfigure the downtown stub terminal of the West Side "L" for construction of the double-deck Wacker Drive. The upper level of the ornate Wells Street Terminal building, located between Jackson Boulevard and Van Buren Street, was removed to allow the West Side "L" to connect directly with the Loop "L." The West Side's historic connection to the Loop "L" at the southwest corner of the structure was removed. Thus, from 1955 to 1958, the Garfield Park Branch accessed the Loop "L" at this new junction (below), seen here looking west as a train passes the new control tower. (Right, CTA; below, Bruce Moffat collection.)

The West Side "L" stood in the way of the planned Congress (now Eisenhower) Expressway, so its tracks were temporarily moved and ultimately rebuilt in the median of the new highway. CTA claimed to pioneer such use of medians, but a suburban line with similar characteristics had been built earlier near Los Angeles. Here workers weld rail joints of the new Congress "L" in 1955. (CTA.)

On June 21, 1958, dignitaries, speakers, musicians, and onlookers celebrate the opening of the new West Side Congress "L." This view looks northeast at the Morgan Street entrance to the Halsted station. In the background, the Garfield Park "L" makes one of its last runs on one of the two tracks still standing from the old four-track Metropolitan main line. The structure was demolished soon thereafter. (CTA, photograph by J. Evans.)

CTA's purchase of Chicago Surface Lines included 3,269 streetcars. Many were PCCs, named after the Electric Railway Presidents' Conference Committee, a group that designed a more comfortable, quieter, and faster-accelerating streetcar in the 1930s. Still, the group's efforts were not enough to save the industry. Above, a famous "Green Hornet" PCC takes the last streetcar run in Chicago on June 21, 1958, turning south at Kinzie and Clark Streets. The streetcar's rapid demise left CTA with 600 relatively new PCCs that had been delivered in 1946–1948. The frugal agency recycled their components to build "L" cars. A CTA employee (inset) works on one of the 570 "L" cars (series 6201-6720 and 1-50) built with trucks, motors, generators, seats, windows, and other salvaged streetcar parts. (CTA.)

An "L" car passes the Stock Yards gate in 1954, three years before the branch closed. By 1951 CTA had cut its workforce in half. By 1960 it had abandoned one-quarter of the "L" system and replaced the entire streetcar network with buses in an effort to control costs and meet the changing transportation needs of its potential customers. (Krambles-Peterson Archive.)

In 1959, the White Sox won their first pennant in 40 years. Huge crowds rode the "L" to World Series games, as seen in this photograph at Thirty-fifth Street on what is now the Green Line. Alas, the White Sox lost to the Los Angeles Dodgers, but they won the World Series in 2005, prompting CTA to decorate a few "L" cars in a vinyl wrap of White Sox pinstripes. (CTA.)

Highway construction stimulated an exodus to the suburbs. Television and air-conditioning kept people home who had ridden the "L" to entertainment venues. Ridership fell from 158 million in 1946 to 123 million in 1960, when this photograph was taken looking east from Western Avenue on the Congress Expressway. It appears to show the automobile's supremacy, but all the westbound automobiles are at a standstill. (CTA.)

CTA further reduced costs by inaugurating one-person operation on the Evanston Line with new cars in 1961. The cars had control cabs with fare boxes at either end that allowed one person to operate the train, handle the doors, and collect fares. The train telephone sent signals through the third rail for communication with the line supervisor. It would take decades for one-person operation to spread systemwide. (CTA.)

Early in CTA history, personnel, medical, legal, insurance, and other records were kept all over the system. This central storage facility was established in 1955 in an old horsecar stable at Division and Western. In 1964, records were moved again to the former West Shops at 3900 West Maypole Avenue, taking up two floors of a city-block-long building. Ultimately, of course, record keeping was computerized. The inset shows CTA's new data and management information center in 1966. (CTA.)

Another dramatic change occurred in supplying electric power to trains. This rotary converter installed at a CTA substation in 1906 served for more than 50 years. The substation converted high-voltage alternating current purchased from Commonwealth Edison and other providers to the 600 volts of direct current needed to run trains. Today this job is handled by modern equipment, still at substations. Increasingly, alternators on "L" cars convert the DC back to AC for auxiliaries, such as lights. With its next car order, the "L" will use AC for propulsion since it allows for smoother accelerating and braking, as well as lower operating and maintenance costs. One thing hardly changed in 100 years is the lowly gravity shoe (inset) for drawing power from the third rail. (CTA.)

Eventually all downtown stub terminals of the four original "L" lines were torn down. This view west from Clark Street toward the Merchandise Mart shows the North Water Street terminal of the old Northwestern "L" being dismantled in 1964. (CTA.)

Speedometers (and air-conditioning) became common on "L" cars in 1964. Speedometers are critical to Automatic Train Control (ATC), a safety system installed starting in 1965 that uses electrical circuits in the tracks to continuously detect trains and relay maximum safe speeds to following trains. If the motorman exceeds the limit and ignores a warning, ATC applies the brakes. It is now used systemwide except on part of the Blue Line. (CTA.)

Despite modernization, the "L" still struggled with old equipment and outdated operating procedures. In "armstrong towers," so-called because they required brute force, towermen threw levers that mechanically moved rods made of heavy pipe reaching all the way to the track switches. By 1971, the Granville tower was staffed only during rush hours to switch Evanston Express trains to and from local tracks. (CTA.)

After the success of the Congress "L," other expressway medians were built to accommodate "L" lines. This 1968 view shows construction of the Ninety-fifth Street terminal of the "L" built down the middle of the new Dan Ryan Expressway that opened in 1969. In 2006, this station was the third busiest, after Chicago on the Red Line and Lake in the Loop. Each handled well over four million riders. (CTA.)

This view southeast in 1968 shows construction of a short subway to carry "L" trains from the end of the old Logan Square "L" a mile to the Kennedy Expressway. Below is the new terminal at Jefferson Park when it opened in 1970. Note this station's intermodal nature, with adjacent bus and commuter railroad facilities. That same year, the suburban population surpassed that of the city, and CTA fare revenues failed to cover operating expenses for the first time. (CTA.)

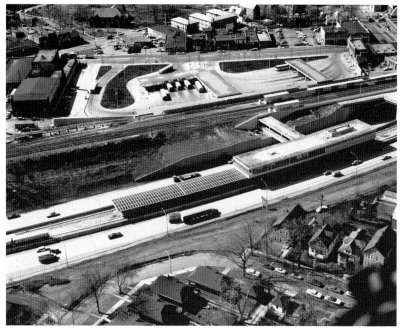

Another station to emphasize intermodal transportation was this modernistic one at Ashland Avenue and Sixty-third Street, opened in 1969. Loomis had been the Englewood Branch's terminal since 1907, but CTA extended the line two blocks west to Ashland Avenue as part of work to build a new car shop and expand the yard. Cantilevers and overhanging roofs reflected the prairie school style of architecture. (CTA.)

Modern "L" cars are 8.5 feet wide and 48 feet long, several feet shorter than the transit norm to handle the tight curves of the Loop "L." Since 1950, they come in "married pairs," generally staying together (for better or worse) throughout their 30-to-40-year lifetimes. This three-couple train heads toward the Loop from Cermak-Chinatown. (CTA.)

Although this photograph was taken considerably earlier, the use of baseball signs on "L" cars continued until the early 1970s. By then, transit systems around the country continued to lose riders and rampant inflation eroded their revenues. The federal government stepped in with funding. In Chicago, the Regional Transportation Authority was created in 1973 as a planning body and to oversee CTA, commuter rail, and suburban buses. (CTA.)

A locomotive shoves empty coal cars south from Lawrence Avenue on April 30, 1973, the last day of freight service. The gauntlet track on the right allowed the wider freight cars to pass "L" stations without tearing up platforms or touching the third rail. (Krambles-Peterson Archive, photograph by J. Buckley.)

Several "L" cars were painted red, white, and blue to celebrate the nation's bicentennial in 1976. They were named after Revolutionary War heroes, including locally popular figures George Rogers Clark, who won the Old Northwest from the British, and Baron von Steuben, who drilled troops at Valley Forge and for whom a Chicago public high school is named. (CTA.)

In 1976, Boeing delivered the first 2400-series cars. When announcing the debut, CTA used its connection with the high-tech company to project a modern image. On the left is George Krambles, CTA general manager. In 2000, Boeing moved its headquarters to Chicago, locating just two blocks from where CTA would headquarter in 2004: 567 West Lake Street. (CTA.)

The "L" reached O'Hare International Airport in 1984. The award-winning terminal designed by Helmut Jahn features undulating, glass-block multicolored walls. Mayor Jane Byrne rushed the project along but her successor, Mayor Harold Washington, got to cut the ribbon. From 1985 to 1997, the "L" experienced a spiral of service cuts, rising fares, and declining ridership. It blamed insufficient public funding. (CTA.)

The "L" suffered a terrible accident on February 4, 1977, at the northeast corner of the Loop "L" during a cold, icy rush hour. A northbound Lake–Dan Ryan train hit a Ravenswood train, and four cars fell off the tracks, killing 11 people. As tragic as this was, there have been extremely few fatalities in the long history of the "L," during which more than 10 billion passengers have ridden. (Krambles-Peterson Archive, photograph by Mike Charnota.)

While service was being extended in other parts of town, the troubled South Side "L" to Jackson Park was being whittled away. The terminus at Stony Island, seen here in 1962, closed in 1982 because of an unsafe bridge over the Illinois Central tracks. This made University the last stop. (CTA.)

In 1993, CTA introduced a color-coded route scheme. It also began phasing out conductors with the introduction of 3200-series cars, which had full-width cabs that allowed operators to open the doors on either side of the train. By 1997, conductors like this one in 1957 were gone, except in the Red and Blue Line subways. This saved CTA $14 million in 1998 alone. Conductors were completely eliminated in 2000. (CTA.)

A line to Midway Airport was announced in 1980, but without funding. Pres. Ronald Reagan found money for it to payback Rep. William Lipinski (D-IL) for his 1986 vote to aid the Nicaraguan contras. The Orange Line opened in 1993, bringing "L" service to the neglected Southwest Side. The Stevenson Expressway median has room for an "L," but the new line instead followed existing railroad rights-of-way. (CTA.)

This 1969 view north shows how the Dan Ryan "L" snaked its way north from Cermak Road, then east at about Eighteenth Street (in the middle of the image) to where it merged with the old South Side "L." Farther north, the line entered the Loop "L" and turned west onto the Lake Street "L." Unfortunately, traffic was lighter on the Lake Street "L" than on the Dan Ryan "L." In 1993, CTA balanced off these routes by pairing the Dan Ryan "L" with the North Side "L" to form the Red Line. At the same time, it paired the Lake Street "L" with the South Side "L" as the Green Line. In 1995, CTA discontinued A/B skip-stop service systemwide, primarily because train frequencies on some lines had declined to a point where longer waits for trains outweighed the time savings from skipping stations. (CTA.)

Since the Green Line paired the two oldest "L"s, it was no surprise that it needed major renovations. To speed up the job, CTA took the unusual step of closing the line during the work, which still took more than two years. The photograph at left, looking east from Clinton, shows why CTA had even considered dismantling the line. The more than $400 million project included replacing structural steel; installing new ties, rails, and signals; and replacing or renovating stations. Below, looking west on Lake Street from Wells Street, shows repainted structures ready for new tracks. In 1997, community opposition to the Green Line along Sixty-third Street led to dismantling the structure east of Cottage Grove. This included tearing down new tracks and a new station at Dorchester. Whether removing the "L" improved the neighborhood, as some predicted, is open to debate. (CTA.)

When "L" transfers originated in 1935, transfer stamping established the time limit for a subsequent ride. Synchronous clocks in these little red machines were the first use of household current in most "L" stations—initially via long extension cords from nearby houses or stores. The practice of punching times on transfers (as they were distributed) obsoleted these machines in 1971. Tokens were introduced in 1950 and retired in 1999. During that period, the fare rose from 18¢ to $1.50 (subsequently to $2). In 1997, magnetic stripe cards began replacing tokens, transfers, and cash. A further improvement came in 2000: a plastic "smart card" with an embedded computer chip. It accepts credit card payments and tax-exempt payroll deductions, and offers speedy "touch and go" boarding. (CTA; inset, Greg Borzo.)

The Pink Line became the eighth route in CTA's palette in 2006. Part of the new line runs over the "Paulina Connector," a previously little-used section of track. A renovated segment of that track is seen in 1964 going off to the left (north) from what used to be the Marshfield Junction of the old Metropolitan "L." (CTA.)

Opposite: This 1911 view north shows that there used to be a station at Clark Junction. It closed in 1949, but a vestige of the platform can still be seen west of the main-line tracks. Southbound express and local trains (running on the left-hand tracks at that time) approach the camera. Other stations that have closed along what is today the Brown Line include: Grand, Oak, Division, Schiller, Larrabee and Ogden, North and Halsted, Willow, Webster, Wrightwood, and Ravenswood (near Wilson). Evidence of former stations is visible along the line such as at North and Halsted, where the tracks spread apart—a sign that a platform once stood between them. (Krambles-Peterson Archive.)

ELEVEN

BROWN LINE TURNS 100

The Brown Line, with 28 stations over 11.3 miles, runs from the Loop to Clark Junction (just north of Belmont) over tracks that were opened in 1900 as part of the Northwestern "L." From there the line heads west, north, and west again, over a 1907 extension to Kimball. This extension defines the unique spirit of the line, so the Brown Line celebrated its 100th anniversary in 2007. That is why it warrants its own chapter in this book.

The Brown Line provides more than one-quarter million rides a week. For these passengers and the many more people who live along the line's path, the centennial was, indeed, something to celebrate. Besides getting people to work, the Brown Line created and continues to help maintain property values along its route. It also gives the neighborhoods it serves a certain character.

In these days of urban revival and traffic gridlock, communities along the Brown Line are experiencing a renaissance, as is the Brown Line itself. Ridership increased 79 percent from 1979 to 2004, making the Brown Line the third-busiest line (after the Red and Blue Lines). During the 1990s, it accounted for most of the growth in "L" ridership systemwide—one reason CTA decided to renovate the line. The $530 million Brown Line Capacity Expansion Project is the biggest renovation of the "L" ever.

The Northwestern "L" first proposed building an extension to the Ravenswood neighborhood at ground level from Wilson. This generated too much opposition, so the line proposed elevated routes, including one from Sheridan along Irving Park Road. A route from Clark was approved in 1905, and construction began the following year, as seen near Newport and Racine Avenues. (Chicago History Museum.)

Clockwise, the structure was built high to cross Chicago and North Western's tracks near Ravenswood Avenue. Farther west, workers clear land for the "L" near Western and Leland Avenues in 1907, when the area was still full of farms and fields. The branch opened to Western on May 18, 1907, and within two months, was carrying 10,000 riders a day. The last mile (Western-Kimball) was built at ground level—to save money—through land owned by the Northwest Land Association. When the association deeded the streets to the city, the ground-level track was grandfathered in. By December 14, 1907, the branch reached the Kimball terminal, seen here near opening day. Western to Kimball was served by a shuttle until 1909, when through service was inaugurated. In this *c.* 1915 view along Lawrence Avenue, the area was already filled with houses and stores. (Above left, Chicago History Museum; above right, Krambles-Peterson Archive; below right, Krambles-Peterson Archive; below left, CTA.)

In 1913, Ravenswood trains started running to the South Side via the Loop "L." Some connected with the Kenwood Branch, but here one approaches the Normal Park Branch terminal on the far South Side. This might seem odd, but the Ravenswood has seen many route configurations. From 1943 to 1949, it even ran through the subway to relieve overcrowding on the Loop "L." (Krambles-Peterson Archive.)

The early success of the Ravenswood Branch required more capacity. Here workers extend platforms at Western in 1925. By then, the once-exclusive railroad suburb of Ravenswood had lost its tranquil character and been swallowed up by Chicago. (CTA.)

134

The original stucco-clad station house, torn down in 1974, featured massive, low-pitched half-timbered gables. The attractive building was designed by Arthur U. Gerber, who designed several other "L" stations. The Terminal Theater was a local landmark from the 1920s until it was demolished in 1964. (Chicago History Museum.)

In the 1950s, CTA tried to stem the loss of riders by opening several park-and-ride lots. The first such lot to charge a fee opened at the Kimball terminal in 1955 with space for 123 cars. "L" patrons paid a quarter to activate the "automatic self-service entrance gate"; non-patrons paid an extra dime. Today 17 stations have park-and-ride lots with more than 6,000 spaces. (CTA.)

A train rounds the bend near Roscoe Street and Ravenswood Avenue heading for the South Side. "Eversharp" on the water tower reveals that the building in the background was a pencil factory. This tower is still decorated with pencils even though the factory was converted into condominiums long ago. (CTA.)

The same curve is seen in this remarkable photograph by Terry Evans, one of Chicago's most noted photographers. Published in *Revealing Chicago: An Aerial Portrait* (Harry N. Abrams, 2005), it illustrates how the "L" threads its way through Chicago, the "City of Neighborhoods," and fits comfortably into the fabric of its surroundings. (Terry Evans.)

CTA faces constant maintenance and upgrading needs. In 1963, it installed new track and a modern interlocking system at the Kimball yard. All replacement materials were prefabricated, and CTA manufactured four turnouts and one diamond crossing in its frog shop at Sixty-first Street and Calumet Avenue. (CTA.)

During the 1950s and 1960s, "L" employees maintained a small nature preserve at the southern end of the Kimball yard. They installed a fish pool, a birdhouse, a rock garden, lilac bushes, fruit trees, a running stream, and a barbecue pit, all set off from the busy tracks and noisy trains by a split-rail fence made of railroad ties. Purple martins settled in the birdhouse, and ducks stopped by for water. (CTA.)

An aerial view north of Belmont in 1964 shows Wrigley Field in the background, before night lights were installed. Sheffield Avenue is on the left, and in the foreground is the Belmont station, with its quaint passenger bridge—a favorite local landmark used for everything from watching trains to proposing matrimony. Today about 1,000 Purple, Red, and Brown Line trains pass through this junction every weekday, making it one of the busiest intersections of the "L." (CTA.)

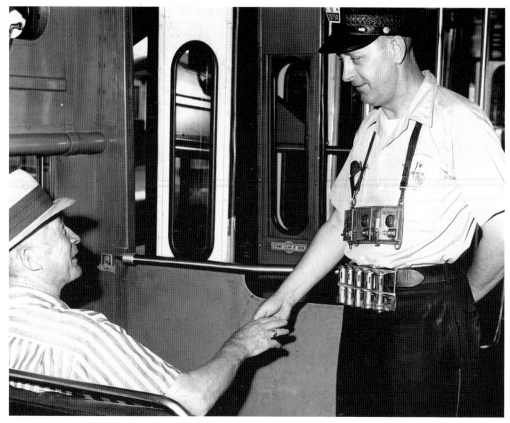

In an effort to reduce costs, CTA stopped staffing some stations during hours of low ridership. This required riders to pay on the train, seen here as a conductor collects fares on the Ravenswood Branch in 1964. The fare register around his neck counts three types of fares. Pay-on-the-train continued on some lines until 1997. (CTA.)

By the 1970s, ridership had plummeted so CTA cut service and closed stations during certain hours of the day. In 1974, a new Kimball terminal got the first piece of art designed for an "L" station, a welded-steel sculpture. It did not survive the 2007 renovation, but original works of art are now found systemwide. In the late 1980s, ridership surged, partly because of neighborhood revitalization along the branch. (Greg Borzo.)

Neighborhood residents apply a fresh coat of paint to the Rockwell Station in 1989 as part of CTA's Adopt-a-Station program. Built in 1907, this was one of many historic "L" stations on the Brown Line, until it was replaced in 2006. The best examples of quaint, original station houses still in operation on this line include Diversey, Armitage, Sedgwick, and Quincy. (CTA.)

Riders might think they were dreaming if they spotted this Airstream trailer on the roof of a building north of Montrose. Architect Edward Noonan of Chicago Associates Planners and Architects used a crane to hoist it there in 1989. The firm uses it as a break room and urban retreat. (Greg Borzo.)

This chapter began with an aerial view of the point where the Ravenswood Branch splits from the North Side main line. It finishes at the other end of the branch with an aerial view north along Kimball Avenue in 1964. Albany Park serves as a port of entry for new Chicagoans, with Asian Americans increasingly settling in the area. Other neighborhoods served by the Brown Line continue to see an influx of families and young professionals as well as escalating property values and increasing "L" ridership. In 2006, the Brown Line carried almost 50,000 riders every weekday, for a total of more than 12 million. Such high numbers led to crowded cars and warranted more capacity, so CTA launched an ambitious renovation scheduled to be completed in 2009. (CTA.)

Opposite: Most worn-out wooden cars were burned, their remaining metal sold as scrap. Railfans were often invited to photograph such events. Here 23 cars were torched at the Skokie Shops in June 1957. Some wood-bodied cars served more than 50 years, much longer than expected. The last one in revenue service ran on December 1, 1957. (CTA.)

TWELVE

MAGIC AND MYSTERY OF THE "L"

The "L" inspires people in many ways. Novelists use it as a setting, and poets are drawn to its riveting past. Nelson Algren called it "the city's rusty heart." Artists photograph or paint its coarse beauty. The "L" was featured on three cows in "Cows On Parade," a popular public art exhibit in 1999. Railfans and rail historians study its every nuance, from the minutia of operating procedures to the life of each piece of rolling stock. Chicago "L".org is a good example of this.

Like the weather, the "L" is a favorite topic of conversation. Some people like to bash the "L," even though it carries them to work every day. This is fed by sensational newspaper headlines such as, "Unintelligible announcements stump CTA riders" and "Prepare for the worst commute of your life."

Other forums, such as "the CTA Tattler," are more balanced. This daily blog reports on the shortcomings of the "L" but also celebrates the big-city spectacle that plays out every day on the stage made up of "L" cars, platforms, and stations. And what a stage it is, where rappers perform for loose change, aldermen ride next to homeless people, bomb-sniffing dogs are commonplace, panhandlers and pickpockets ply their trades, and dozens of languages are readily overheard. This spectacle can be observed around the clock every day of the year, at least on the Red and Blue Lines.

The "L" is both old and dynamic, ever changing. The Loop structure and dozens of stations are officially designated historic landmarks. Meanwhile, CTA has shown creativity in using original artwork to decorate renovated stations on the Blue Line, and in building a world-class station at Roosevelt Road with a science decor reflecting the nearby Museum Campus in the spacious underground connection between the subway and the "L."

Some wooden cars were converted to non-passenger service, such as work trains. Here about 20 cars taken off their wheels are used to store parts and equipment at the Skokie Shops in 1959. Wooden cars were used for storage, offices, and locker rooms at many terminals and yards into the 1980s. (CTA.)

In 1903, the Aurora Elgin and Chicago inaugurated newspaper trains on the Metropolitan "L" to whisk the latest news to the suburbs. By 1910, these loading facilities had been built at the Met's downtown terminal. Here in 1920, workers load a North Shore passenger car converted to the service. Newspaper trains operated on the "L" until 1947. (Bruce Moffat collection.)

Early on, some "L" lines allowed smoking on cars designated with a "Smoker" sign on the side and an S on each end. Such cars doubled as informal men's clubs. The worldwide 1917–1919 influenza epidemic that killed 20 million to 40 million people prompted a smoking ban on the "L" in 1918, and that prohibition continues to this day. (Krambles-Peterson Archive.)

On November 1, 1915, at Jackson Park these five ladies boarded a "fresh air car" with many of its windows locked open to maximize air circulation. The "L" operated one such car on certain trains between Jackson Park and Evanston at the city's behest to fight an influenza outbreak. These ladies seem to have heeded an advertisements inside the car that read, "Get the fresh air habit; dress warm enough to enjoy it." Another said, "Too much fresh air is just enough." It is not known how long these cars operated, but the idea that fresh, lakefront air would promote good health was widespread—and well founded, given the horrendous quality of Chicago's air in the early 20th century. (Chicago History Museum.)

This poster is one of the best-known artistic depictions of the "L." In the 1920s, CRT and other Samuel Insull–owned properties commissioned more than 200 such posters to encourage the use of transit for more than just going to work. Ironically this is the only one of the advertisements featuring the "L" itself. Of course, the original *c.* 1926 poster did not mention CTA; it said, "Rapid Transit Lines, Fast . . . Reliable." This version was created in 1997 to celebrate the 100th anniversary of the Loop "L." (Poster Plus, Chicago.)

The Strauss Yielding Barrier Company and railroad officials demonstrate a curious crossing barrier made of steel netting at Austin Avenue on the Douglas Park Branch in 1921. It worked well enough to remain in use for three decades but was not duplicated elsewhere on the "L." (CTA.)

The Met's funeral trains, which operated between 1906 and 1934, gave new meaning to "end of the line." The charter trains served Mount Carmel, Concordia, Oak Ridge, and Waldheim cemeteries in the western suburbs. In 1907, the Met rebuilt this passenger car with stained-glass windows, seating for 30 mourners, and a large door to accommodate the casket(s). It even installed casket elevators at Laflin, Hoyne, and its downtown terminal. (CTA.)

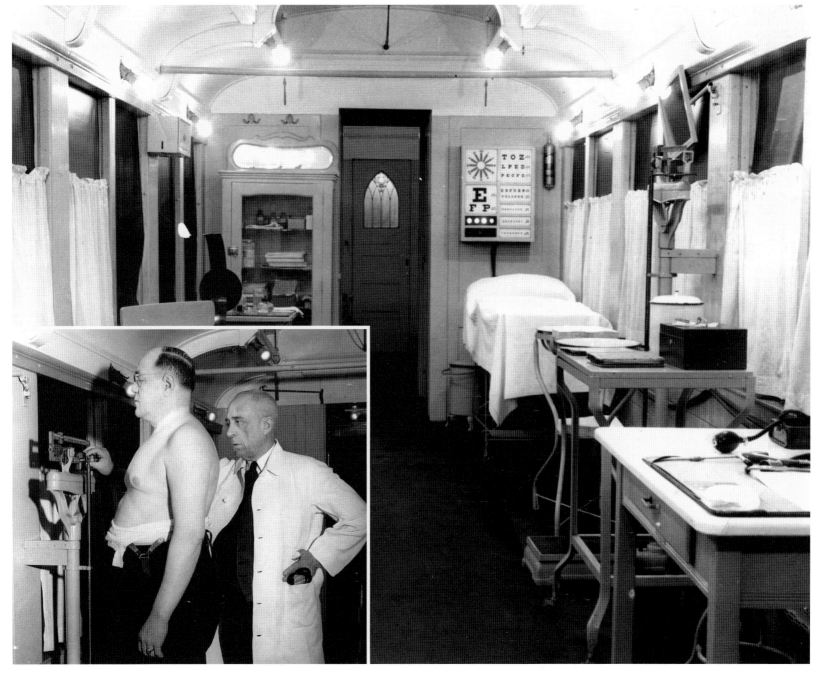

Dozens of funerals were handled per week in 1907, but only 11 in all of 1933. By then, roads were better and automobiles could readily carry mourners to cemeteries. In 1922, CRT converted funeral car 756 into a medical clinic. Still, the stained-glass window in the door gave away the car's previous purpose. This car, perhaps the most unusual one in "L" history, was scrapped in 1953. (CTA.)

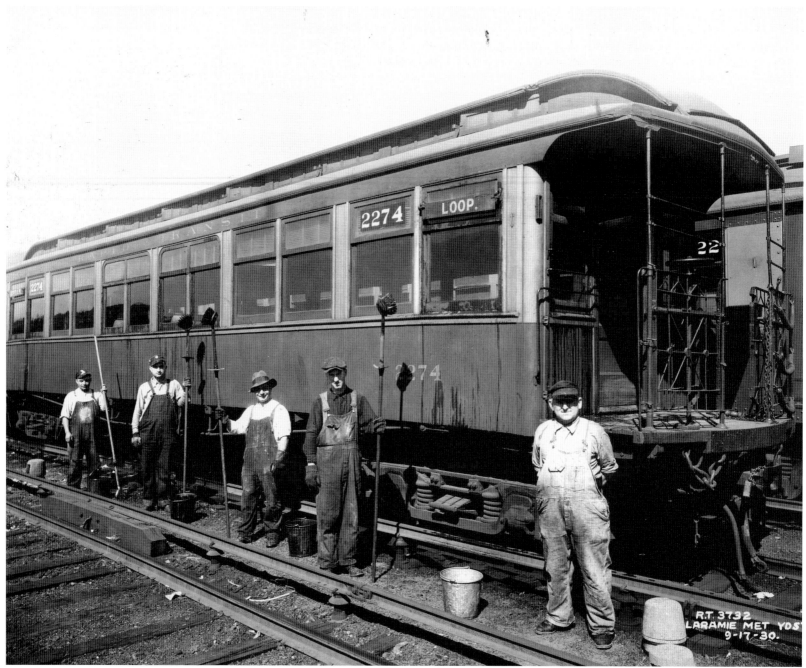

Early on, most tasks on the "L" were extremely labor intensive, from construction to fare collection. In 1930, a crew at the Laramie yard washes a car manually. (CTA.)

Thirty-two years later, the "L" purchased and installed this automated car wash at the Des Plaines Shops for $45,000. It could wash 20 cars an hour. "A simple touch of buttons set in motion the mechanism . . . for a quick bath and scrub-down," read promotional materials. Despite extensive automation, labor still accounts for about three-quarters of the expenses of the "L." (CTA.)

Shirley Temple, America's top-grossing box office star of the 1930s, took the controls of this "L" in 1938. It is easy to imagine her singing "The Good 'L' Lollipop" to motorman Charles Blade. (CTA.)

Subway construction attracted much attention, including tours and events such as this Kiwanis luncheon on the Clark platform of the Dearborn Street subway in August 1941—10 years before the line even opened. The subway was one of Chicago's cooler spots before air-conditioning was common. (CTA.)

Years ago, boys dreamed of getting model trains for Christmas. For Chicagoans, what better model to get than an "L" car? This whimsical drawing graced the December 1954 cover of *Transit News*, a CTA employee publication. Since the early 1990s, CTA has operated a popular Santa train: six decorated cars, plus a flatcar carrying Santa and his sleigh. Another holiday tradition is penny rides on New Year's Eve. (CTA.)

In May 1948, CTA used this 4,000-gallon tank car to wash the State Street subway's five miles of concrete walls, floors, and ceilings. The job took 10 nights during off-peak hours. It is not known how effective this cleaning was, but in the summer the same car was used to spray weeds with herbicide. CTA wages a constant battle against litter and graffiti. The "Litter-Getter," a portable gas-powered vacuum, not only sucked up paper, bottles, cans, and other debris but also ground up the debris for disposal. The 1,800-pound unit, seen here at Halsted on the Congress "L" in 1961, required four workers to handle and was moved station to station on a flatcar. (CTA.)

Often dirty and unsightly, the space under the "L" can also be attractive or at least useful. Clockwise, a man tinkers with his car under the shade of the Douglas Park Branch. In the early 1980s, Ed Gandy created a parklike setting for renters of his buildings along the Ravenswood "L" on Cleveland Avenue. The awning over the raised patio covers a barbecue-equipped bar. CTA leases land under the "L" for a nominal fee, but leaseholders must keep it clean. Stores are also located under tracks and in stations, such as the ones in this 1928 view of Halsted on the Englewood Branch. In 2003, CTA rented space to 27 businesses under the Brown and Red Lines, the only lines still renting such space. These stores typically have a unique character—and reduced rent to compensate for the noise. For motorists, however, the "L" darkens streets and inhibits traffic. (CTA.)

John Kalinowski silk-screens baseball signs at the Skokie Shops around 1967. With "Wrigley Field" and "Comiskey Park" (now U.S. Cellular Field) on either side, the signs were carried on the front of North-South and West-South "L" trains into the 1970s. On game days, "L" trains are crowded and festive—especially when the hometown team wins. (CTA.)

This escalator at State and Van Buren Streets, along with another at State and Lake Streets, went into service in 1967. The aluminum and Plexiglas enclosure probably did not win any architectural awards, but "L" patrons must have been happy to get some help with the stairs. How long the structures survived Chicago's weather extremes is unknown. (CTA.)

This beautiful view east on the Chicago River in 1971 catches a ship sailing in front of the double-deck Wells Street bridge carrying two "L" trains. The ship was part of Chicago's summertime lakefront festival. (CTA.)

Most freight trains on the "L" ran at night to avoid busy daylight hours. In 1965, switchman Carl Lyday uses a fusee to signal the motorman to stop so this coal car would be left in the proper spot for unloading at the Lill Coal Company. Coal was the top cargo by weight, averaging 300 tons per night in the 1940s. The "L" also carried lumber, flour, lube oil, ice, and even World War II priority items for the government. (CTA.)

Juris Graudins, a former CTA employee, used discarded CTA destination signs and advertisement cards in his class at Fenner Elementary School in the Cabrini-Green public housing project during the summer of 1974. He found that the advertisements and signs motivated students to improve their reading skills—as well as their skills getting around the city. (CTA.)

When the "L" still accepted tokens and cash, counting and securing the coins was a huge job. In the 1970s, all this work was handled at CTA's central counting department at Seventy-seventh Street and Vincennes Avenue. These workers had to wear pocketless jumpsuits. And in the days of exact change and locking fare boxes, the CTA had to process the money quickly to avoid tying up the city's coin supply. (CTA.)

Calamity often strikes the "L." Clockwise, 88 inches of snow fell with hardly any melting during the 1978–1979 winter, one of Chicago's worst. This January scene at Davis in Evanston shows an "L" car with an improvised plywood snowplow. Such plows failed to prevent service disruptions. In 1957, Chicago's biggest thunderstorm in 72 years flooded the "L" from the Congress subway portal east of Halsted Street all the way north to Jackson. Water poured eastward along the construction site into the unfinished subway. The LaSalle station had 12 feet of water. The temporarily relocated Garfield Park "L" operates to the left, unimpeded by the flood. A strike in 1979 led to this crowd on the Belmont platform. In 1996, a five-alarm fire destroyed the vacant Wilson Shop and adjacent yard. At its peak, 42 pieces of fire equipment fought the blaze, which disrupted service for several days. (CTA.)

Chicago Cubs hall of famer and local hero Ernie Banks greets CTA workers who had put in a lot of overtime during the record snowfall in January 1979. Banks was on the CTA board from 1969 to 1981. The board comprises seven people, three appointed by the governor and four by the mayor, which gives the mayor control. (CTA.)

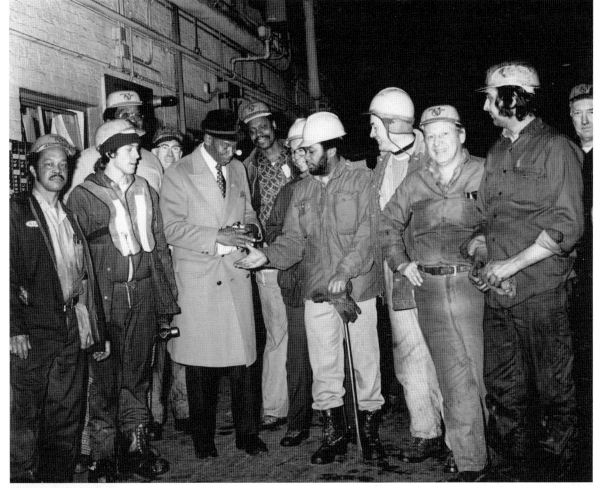

Arline Datu and Daniel Kane, two one-time CTA employees, celebrate their wedding on October 16, 1977, during a reception trip on an antique train chartered by friends. Many people pursue love and romance on the "L." "Cutie on the Brown Line" read one of the "I Saw You" advertisements in the *Chicago Reader* in February 2005. (CTA.)

The Clarke House, the city's oldest building, was constructed in 1836 "in the country" at Sixteenth Street and Michigan Avenue. By 1872 Chicago had engulfed the area, so the house was moved to Forty-fifth Street and Wabash Avenue. A century later the city decided to return it to near its original location, which required moving it over the "L" at Forty-fourth Street. On December 4, 1977, the house was jacked up and pulled across the tracks. When the hydraulic equipment froze, the house could not be lowered for two weeks until the weather warmed up. Here it waits to be lowered. Today the Clarke House is part of the Prairie Avenue Historic District. Nearby at Illinois Institute of Technology's campus center, an acoustic tube dampens the noise of Green Line trains passing overhead. (Left, Chicago Department of Cultural Affairs; below, Greg Borzo.)

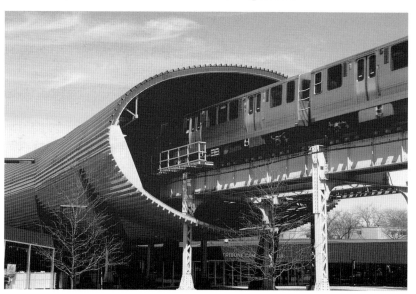

Bicycles have a long history on the "L." During a nationwide bike boom in the 1890s, the South Side "L" allowed bikes in the front car of each train. Around the same time, the Metropolitan "L" provided bike racks at some stations. In 2000, CTA began to allow two bikes per car, except during rush hour. Karen Shinners of the Chicago Cycling Club demonstrates the concept. The "L" inspires whimsy, and one highlight on the Red Line is a bicycle on the roof of Uptown (formerly Urban) Bikes that lights up when an "L" train passes at night. The store owner wanted to locate near the "L" and could hardly have chosen better; 4653 North Broadway is between Lawrence and Wilson, two of the closest stations on the entire system. (Right, CTA; below, Greg Borzo.)

Scores of movies use the "L" to create a gritty urban setting or to establish the location as Chicago. Clockwise, Diane Keaton seems to be reviewing her lines as *Looking for Mr. Goodbar* is filmed in December 1976. In *Code of Silence*, Chuck Norris plays a cop fighting corruption in the big city. Handling his own stunts in this 1985 film, he fights with a bad guy on top of a train equipped with a special running platform. In the best scene, Norris dives from the top of an "L" car as it crosses the Chicago River over the Wells Street bridge. In *Running Scared*, another cop movie filmed in 1985, Billy Crystal and Gregory Hines chase a limousine in their Yellow Cab right on the tracks. The chase scene is reason enough to see this fast-paced comedy. (CTA.)

If the Motion Picture Academy gave an Oscar for best special effects on the "L," it would go to *Spiderman 2*. Although Spiderman lives in a generic big city like New York, the elevated scenes in this movie either were filmed on the Chicago "L" or are computer enhancements, shots for which Universal Studios bought the body of car 2258 and chartered a train that ran through the Loop. The best scenes involve Spiderman fighting Doctor Octopus in and on top of an "L" and then summoning all his powers to handle the runaway train. Other great movies featuring the "L" include *While You Were Sleeping*, *The Fugitive*, *The Blues Brothers*, *Cooley High*, *Just Visiting*, and *Risky Business*. (Kobal collection.)

The "L" also figures prominently in many television programs, such as *Early Edition, Chicago Hope,* and *ER. The Last Leaf,* a made-for-television movie starring Art Carney in 1983, converted the intersection of the North Side "L" and Armitage Avenue into a stop along New York's Greenwich Street elevated line—the nation's first elevated rail transit line (see pages 17 and 18). (CTA.)

Models strutted down the aisle of a specially appointed Brown Line train on April 30, 2006, when Nova Art Fair organized a fashion show to help emerging artists. Here a model shows off a lollipop-dispensing dress. Incidentally, the long board behind her left hand is a gangplank for evacuating passengers. There is one (or a specialty ladder) at the rear of every alternate "L" car. (Tobey Geise, Fig Media.)

In 1976, CTA sent its first pair of new 2400-series cars out for publicity shots. Employees were invited to bring family members so the cars would look full. George Krambles (with the hat) took or collected many of the photographs in this book. CTA general manager/executive director from 1976 to 1980, Krambles was a great friend to transit professionals and railfans. His nephew Art Peterson continues the tradition. (CTA.)

South Side Rapid Transit Car 1, built in 1892, was preserved by CTA and now resides at the Chicago History Museum as the centerpiece of the Chicago: Crossroads of America permanent exhibit. A crane lifted the car into a special second-floor entrance in January 2006. Visitors can walk through and sit in the relic—the only remaining car from the first fleet of the "L." (Chicago History Museum, photograph by John Alderson.)

EPILOGUE

Where one stands on the "L" depends on where one sits. A rider caught in one of the recent derailments or fires might focus on safety issues, deteriorating service, and deferred maintenance. A CTA official, however, would be proud that "L" ridership has increased in eight of the past nine years, with a 4.5 percent jump in 2006—and that the "L" had the lowest operating expense per revenue vehicle mile (as well as per revenue hour) of the six largest U.S. rail transit systems.

No doubt, the "L" suffers from a shortage of operating and capital funds, for which it must fight with the suburbs. At the same time, the ongoing $282 million Red Line and $530 Brown Line renovations suggest that the "L" will continue to find what it needs to survive.

In fact, the "L" is poised to expand. Several extensions and new lines are under consideration. The Circle Line, a large semicircle around downtown connecting several existing lines, appears to be the most likely next addition to the system because its critical "alternatives analysis" is furthest along of all proposals. The following extensions are also on the table: Red Line to Roseland, Pullman, or 130th Street, all on the far South Side; Orange Line to Ford City shopping center; Yellow Line to Old Orchard shopping center in Skokie; and Express service to O'Hare and Midway Airports from a new "super station" now under construction at 108 North State Street.

In addition, some say the "L" should serve the Museum Campus, Navy Pier, and McCormick Place, three of the city's biggest attractions. Of course, any expansion depends on additional funding, which has been notoriously difficult to acquire. In fact, in the past two years, CTA diverted $60 million in capital funds to cover operating deficits.

Things could get worse before they get better. CTA estimates that it needs $8 billion in capital over the next five years to meet all transit needs, and an additional $2 billion to include all planned rail line extensions. Meanwhile, its $1.1 billion budget for 2007 includes an operating deficit that may lead to deep service cuts and steep fare increases on the "L." Citing a chronic shortage of public funds for operating and capital needs, the RTA and CTA call 2007 the "Year for Decision" about transit and the Chicago "L."

BIBLIOGRAPHY

Chicago's Rapid Transit: Volume 1, Rolling Stock, 1892–1947. Chicago: Central Electric Railfans' Association, 1973.

Cudahy, Brian. *Destination: Loop.* Brattleboro, VT: Stephen Greene Press, 1982.

Duis, Perry. *Challenging Chicago.* Urbana, IL: University of Illinois Press, 1998.

Franch, John. *Robber Baron: The Life of Charles Tyson Yerkes.* Urbana, IL: University of Illinois Press, 2006.

Hilton, George. *The Cable Car in America.* Berkeley, CA: Howell North Books, 1971.

Hornung, Clarence. *Wheels Across America.* New York: A. S. Barnes and Company, 1959.

Krambles, George, and Art Peterson. *CTA at 45.* Oak Park, IL: George Krambles Transit Scholarship Fund, 1993.

Lind, Alan. *Chicago Surface Lines.* Park Forest, IL: Transport History Press, 1974.

Miller, Donald. *City of the Century.* New York: Touchstone, 1996.

Moffat, Bruce. *The "L."* Chicago: Central Electric Railfans' Association, 1995.

Reed, Robert. *The New York Elevated.* Cranbury, NJ: A. S. Barnes and Company, 1978.

Wasik, John. *Merchant of Power.* New York: Palgrave Macmillian, 2006.

www.Chicago–L.org

www.TransitChicago.com

Young, David. *Chicago Transit.* DeKalb, IL: Northern Illinois University Press, 1998.

ACROSS AMERICA, PEOPLE ARE DISCOVERING
SOMETHING WONDERFUL. *THEIR HERITAGE.*

Arcadia Publishing is the leading local history publisher in the United States. With more than 3,000 titles in print and hundreds of new titles released every year, Arcadia has extensive specialized experience chronicling the history of communities and celebrating America's hidden stories, bringing to life the people, places, and events from the past. To discover the history of other communities across the nation, please visit:

www.arcadiapublishing.com

Customized search tools allow you to find regional history books about the town where you grew up, the cities where your friends and family live, the town where your parents met, or even that retirement spot you've been dreaming about.